Spence Spencer

The scenery of Ithaca and the Head Waters of the Cayuga Lake

Spence Spencer

The scenery of Ithaca and the Head Waters of the Cayuga Lake

ISBN/EAN: 9783337142377

Printed in Europe, USA, Canada, Australia, Japan

Cover: Foto ©Andreas Hilbeck / pixelio.de

More available books at **www.hansebooks.com**

STEEPLE ROCK ON BUTTERMILK CREEK, ITHACA

THE
SCENERY OF ITHACA

AND THE

Head Waters of the Cayuga Lake,

AS

PORTRAYED BY DIFFERENT WRITERS,

AND EDITED

By THE PUBLISHER.

ITHACA, N. Y.:
SPENCE SPENCER.
1866.

TO THE

HON. EZRA CORNELL.

The Publisher dedicates this Book to one whose name will ever be known and honored throughout the State; to one who has done so much for the welfare of Ithaca; who has done and is still doing so much to improve and beautify it, and whose name and memory will here be remembered and cherished for the many kindnesses to individuals, "the small sweet courtesies of life," as well as commemorated by the Grand College Halls that are here to be reared, and which will make his name a household word to future generations.

Those who visit Ithaca, see in and around it everything to constitute it a great summer resort. They visit Taghkanic, Lucifer, Fall-Creek, Buttermilk, Lick-Brook, Cascadilla; walk through the wild ravines, climb the rugged rocks, or sail on the silvery Cayuga, and say that Ithaca possesses more scenery, wild and beautiful, and well worth seeing, than any other place in the State.

The Publisher of this book has procured descriptions of these resorts, and hopes that this work will fall into the hands of thousands who seek recreation and amusement in travel in the summer season. It is proper for him to say also, that the articles, having in most part been written by different individuals, who seem to have been inspired by the same thought, some repetition, both of ideas and words, has been unavoidable.

OUR SCENERY.

Rome boasted of her seven hills, from whose throne of beauty she ruled the world. Ithaca makes her boast of seven streams, concerning which she challenges the world. Each of these has a character of beauty peculiar to itself, so that they must all be seen to comprehend the perfect whole. Enfield is distinguished by its giddy winding walk along the sides of the profound precipices. The Ravine of Lick-Brook is as utterly wild as on the day when Ithaca was a log-cabin under the hill; on the contrary, the explorer of Six Mile Creek emerges at brief intervals into the sight of farm houses and cultivated fields. The interest of Taghkanic mainly centers in its magnificent Fall, 215 feet in height; whereas the Cascadilla, as its beautiful name imports, is remarkable for its numerous smaller though not less picturesque cascades, not many of them rising to the dignity and sublimity of falls. Fall Creek is distinguished by its broad and unfailing stream, which at all seasons goes sounding through its almost impassible gorge and casts itself headlong over the nearest and noblest of all our cataracts, the Ithaca Fall.

Contrasted with this, is the untastefully, though not unaptly named, Buttermilk Ravine, where the stream is so shallow and at the same time distributes itself so widely over the rocks as to partake the foamy whiteness belonging to the product of the churn rather than of the spring.

If you find yourself in the social mood, pile up a "democrat"* with genial, laughter-loving friends, and go to Goodwin's. If your "soul is dark," take a sun-shiny day, and wander among the woodland paths that border the Cascadilla, or through the Ravine of Buttermilk. If you feel that you need to be sobered and solemnized, if you yearn for what Thoreau calls "the wild," if your poetry has gone to seed, and your bump of veneration is flattening apace, hie to Fall Creek, and spend an hour on its overhanging cliffs, listening to the boom of the cataract, or lose thyself in the twilight shade and primeval solitudes of Lick-Brook. If you want a pleasant, varied stroll, without being burdened with any particular object except to enjoy a good walk hand in hand with nature, take your lunch and book, say Thoreau's Excursions, or Bryant, or Thompson's Seasons, or Isaac Walton (though I will not promise any fishing), and explore the Six Mile Creek. You are always safe in going to Enfield, if it does not rain, though experience has demonstrated to the writer that from 4 to 6 of a summer afternoon is the hour of extra enjoyment. It is essential in visiting Enfield, it may be well to remark in this place, to conclude with a repast of broiled chickens previously ordered at the inn, and to return by the lower or inlet road. If you have time to visit or to take your friends to visit only one ravine, choose Enfield by all means, as combining the largest combination of striking and interesting features. If two, add Fall Creek. Then Buttermilk. If so happy as to visit four or five, let Taghkanic and the Cascadilla come next in their order. Lick-Brook should not be put

---

* The Ithaca name for a particular kind of open three or four seated wagon, much affected by excursionists in these parts.

later than the sixth, and, if you can possibly spare a day longer, and wish to leave in a vigorous physical condition, do not neglect to trace the windings of Six Mile Creek.

There are ingenious literary manufacturers who roll out from their mills legendary lore by the yard or piece, and will invent you a legend as readily as another class will furnish the resident of Petroleum Square, or the great house of Shoddy, with a venerable coat of arms. We have, as yet, favored this enterprising guild with no orders, so that our wilds may seem singularly destitute of that mossy and ruinous charm which tradition imparts. There have been, doubtless, the usual number of lover's leaps, and Indian maiden's rocks, and sybil's caves, *et id omne genus*. In fact, some of these, on account of their wide fame and authenticity, have been admitted into these pages. But, in the most part, we have preferred to leave these things to the delightful exercise of the tourist's invention. The little we know of the aboriginal Ithacans is mainly confined to doubtful reminiscence of border raids.

And in later days how could we tell, save if some little bird had whispered them to us, the tales of love and disappointment, of questions put and answered which have narrowed life into a dark ravine or expanded it into a sunny landscape? What legends are comparable to the merry reports of pic-nic parties, dancing in the wildwood or ignominiously caught in showers, and crouching under rocks and trees? What so sad and suggestive as the chapter of accidents which have shadowed some of these glens, where a single heedless step has produced irreparable and eternal consequences. It rejoices me to think how many a burdened spirit has cast off its load in these calm, unworldly scenes; how many a mind has gathered the inspiration which reäppeared in verse, or painting, or scholarship, or, better yet, a refined nature and a holy life; how many a thought of beauty or of peace has been wafted on the spray of these waterfalls, or gathered by a spiritual geology from these worn and ancient rocks. For hath not old Burton, maundering in his quaint and learned talk, said, " Truth is no doctoresse, she takes no degrees at Paris or Oxford, among great clerks, disputants, subtle Aristotles, men *nodose ingenii*, able to take Sully by the chin. But oftentimes to such a one as myself, an idiota or private person, no great things, melancholizing in woods where waters are, quiet places by rivers, fountains (whereas the silly man, expecting no such matter, thinketh only how best delectate and refresh his mynde continually with nature, her pleasant scenes, woods, waterfalls), on a sudden the goddess herself, truth, has appeared with a silvering light and a sparkling countenance, so as yo may not be able lightly to resist her."

Some of the sketches of scenery in this volume may perchance seem to the general reader tediously minute. But after a little practical experience of rambling among our glens, this will no longer be an objection. The writer remembers so keenly the unnecessary delay and fatigue undergone by himself in experimenting, before he had learned the most direct and easiest paths, and even the most attractive scenes, that he desires to mark out the way so clearly step by step, that "the way-faring man, though a fool, need not err therein." Consequently these sketches have been written, paper and pencil in hand, on the spot. How far he has succeeded in that which constitutes his humble ambition, viz: to furnish a trustworthy guide, who shall smooth the tourist's path and heighten his appreciation of these grand and lonely scenes, without needlessly obtruding himself or his rhetoric, the practical test alone must decide.

In this labor of love, taken from the gravest and highest of all duties, we have been governed by no vulgar commercial motive of advertising our village. The God of Nature forbid that we should "stick our bills" in sacrilegious defacement upon such works of his own hand as these. Our motive is drawn from the veritable rapture with which our astonished eyes first looked upon the scenery of Ithaca and its environs, and the inexhaustible and growing resources which we have found in these beautiful retreats for the recuperation both of a wearied mind and body, and for the repose, culture and exaltation of the spirit. So satisfied have we been in the consciousness of our "hidden treasures," that we have made an effort to display them to the world. But the time has come when we must send out into the highways and invite all the lovers of nature to share with us, that our joy may be the more full. If in our instinctive shrinking from all vain-glorious boastings, and from aught which might savor of the showman's panegyric, we have done injustice to our scenery, we will at least secure the satisfaction of hearing the remark common among the visitors to our locality, "The half was not told us."

NOTE.—It may be well to remark that there are springs on this stream, both sulphur and chalybeates.

FALL CREEK.

BY REV. F. N. ZABRISKIE.

Reader, can you climb? And have you a day to spare? Then furnish yourself with "provend" alike for the body and for the mind, but no more than you can stow into the compass of coat pocket or knapsack; encase your feet in thick soled boots, far more suited to pilgrim than "sandal shoon," though less poetical; and let your Jehu drive you down Aurora street to the manufacturing suburbs known as Fall Creek. Thence across the bridge which spans the stream of that name on the Auburn road.

FALL CREEK.   15

Leave your carriage the instant you are over the bridge, and turn short around to your right, up the footpath which ascends the north bank of Fall Creek. You will have gone but a few steps when you stand upon one of those platforms which nature always provides for seeing her waterfalls, and the first and grandest of our cataracts is rolling its white flood before your eyes. You are astonished at the impressiveness which a few yards nearer view has imparted.

The Fall, from the bridge, was like some quiet picture. Here you feel the wild rush and roar of its headlong waters, and catch the thrill of its restless life. If you be so fortunate as to visit the spot just after a freshet, you will see a scene which no equal section of Niagara can surpass, so vast the volume of water, so dark and sullen its hue, besides its peculiar efflorescent appearance as it breaks against the ragged cliff in its descent, the lofty column of spray which rises like the smoke of a conflagration at its foot, almost hiding the entire front of the Fall, and above all the gorgeous rainbow spanning the stream from side to side, and rising in a perfect arch higher than the Fall itself. The water is rarely so low but that the rocks are covered with a snow white and flowing veil, like some fair bride of nature. The height of the Fall (which is known as the Ithaca Fall par excellence), cannot be much less than a hundred and fifty feet, and the breadth fully as much.

It comes pouring through a deep and shadowy defile of towering cliffs, on which the tall pines stand as sentinels, and to whose sides cling the sure-footed chamois of the vegetable kingdom. At its foot lies a deep, dark pool, deep enough to drown a man at all seasons.

The close observer at Taghkanic notices that the water assumes in falling the slope of Indian arrow-heads. By reason of the jagged nature of the rocks down which it pours, the water of this Fall is picturesquely broken up, as if a hundred small cascades were set like gems in one great frame. These unwrought gems are of every shape and of various hues. I am reminded of Aaron's mystic breast-plate, and find a Urim and Thummim here also, on the breast of nature, God's most ancient high priest to man. But I will not be so presumptuous as to attempt describing a waterfall. A flood of words can never represent a flood of waters, and not even the pencil of a Church can more than give the shadow of its terrible beauty. So we will move on to the second scene of this our first act.

Continue along the verge of the bank about fifty feet further, and you stand upon another platform, affording a still finer view. Here the mills and the village have passed out of sight, and shut in by the trees on every side except that which opens toward the Falls, is a place to lie and dream the summer's day away. Once more, if you love the spice which danger lends to enjoyment (though not danger to him who takes heed to his feet), pursue the self same path as far as you can go, and the third scene opens upon you, finest view of all. The Fall has continued to grow in impressiveness in geometrical ratio to your approach, and seems taller and broader, and its voice of greeting more deafening. On your left is an amphitheatre formed by perpendicular rocks, which rise three or four hundred feet from the bed of the stream. At your feet lies the dark, deep tarn. Opposite, the bright green cedars cover the face of the rocky wall. The giant palisade, which stretches northward from the cataract, towers far above all the rest, and wears upon its beetling brow a shaggy garland of evergreens. Behind you, the valley beginning to open on the view, the willow

avenue stretching almost across it, and the high and fertile hills closing in the picture.

We now return along the narrow foot-path, and find that "*facilis est descensus.*" Nor are we timid now, for the near communion of the waterfall has imparted a tonic to the nerves and baptized us into the spirit of adventure. We return to the first stand-point from which we viewed the Fall, and ascend by a foot-path through the chestnuts, oaks and evergreens that cover the cliff above us. Stop and rest occasionally, if you would retain your strength for future effort. And you can well afford to pause, for there is unfolding behind you a fine view of the village and the valley. Nature, as usual, helps the climber with roots and twigs, and saplings forming railings and balusters ready to your hand exactly where they are needed. When you have reached the top I hear you shout, as when Xenophon's Greeks discovered the sea, the Lake! the Lake! For directly in front of you, like a broad and sunny panorama, lie the waters of Cayuga, reflecting the sky and the outline of its own shores, with perhaps a distant sail dotting its surface, or a steam boat gliding noiselessly on its way. Nothing can exceed the tranquil beauty of the water, or the rich and varied coloring of its shadowy shores. The proportion of woodland and cultivated field is perfect, and the contrasts of light and shade, as the shores fade away in the distance, may well heal and cure the weary eye, alike of the cobwebs of study and the jaundice of the gold fever. The peculiarly beautiful picture presented by the lake here, is due partly to the fact that nothing is seen but the lake itself and its accessories, and partly to the incomparable foreground, the effect of which can only be appreciated by being seen.

You follow up the narrow tongue of land from which

you have been looking, and now you have reached the summit, along which, with mounting soul and body, you have been clambering. Look down. Let not your head whirl, though the gorge below you be four or five hundred feet deep. If oratorical, exercise your gifts of utterance from this magnificent rostrum, and out roar the cataract. If nervous, hurry on the descending path. In a moment you stand amid the shaggy gardens of pines and cedars, which we saw crowning the precipice. I need not describe the sensations of this giddy standing-place, as you look down upon the steady plunge of the water over the rocks below.

You pursue your path along the ravine's edge, treading a pavement of rocks hundreds of feet thick. Soon you reach a jutting precipice, on which a solitary pine stands sentinel, and in which the vast fissures and crevices threaten sooner or later a gigantic disruption. This is nature's platform for viewing the second Fall. Deep-seated in the evergreen woods, we call this the Forest Fall. It is at a bend of the stream, where the rocks above rise very high and near together. Though not half as high as the Ithaca Fall, it is still very satisfactory and impressive, having the advantage of a wilder scene and the full volume of the stream. As we pass on, there are three or four other points from which it can be seen to advantage each time, with an almost kaleidescopic change of appearance.

Still mounting up, like the eagles, we soon come in sight of the third Cataract. This is about as high as the Forest Fall, but totally different in other respects. The water just where it flows over the precipice, forms a little island. The two streams thus made are forced into a narrow pass by the conformation of the rocks down which they tumble. The result is, that the poor water is tortured and lashed into a condition of boiling rage and frothing whiteness, which will justify the name we propose for it of the Foaming Fall. The Rapids between this and Forest Fall are exceedingly wild and swift, the bed of the stream being filled with fallen trees and huge boulders from the rocks above.

Pass on till you reach a rude fence or hedge, and enter a low and tangled copse of pine and hemlock. The gleam of our Fourth Fall flashes upon your sight and its regular thunder-beat rises to your ear. Now descend to the bed of the stream. The path is not at all difficult, and you will be richly repaid by the wild and sylvan beauty of the scene. I need not describe it to those who visit it, and I am unable to depict it adequately to those who do not. The Cataract from the successive ledges of rocks over which it glides we will name the Rocky Fall.

Your way now lies along the rocky stairs and sidewalk formed by the edge of the stream, if the water be low. If not you will be obliged (unless you are prepared to do a little wading) to clamber up the rocks again just above the Fall. In this "scramble" I commend you to the good offices of some very friendly roots and saplings, which crook their arms and stretch out their hands for the behest of poor pilgrims. Pass under the foot of the perpendicular rock which you reach at the height of about 40 feet. A few rods farther on your way descend once more to the bed of the stream and will find no more difficulty in wild and beautiful glen. Presently the sides of the Ravine close above you in towering and rocky walls and a distant boom tells you of your approach to another Cataract, and suddenly as you pass a bend of the stream, you come in sight of one of the most beautiful spots of Ithaca scenery. You stand in a vast amphitheatre of frowning rocks. Through a narrow opening at the farther end with a downright plunge, and a prodigious rising of foam at its base, the whole volume of Fall Creek pours. The rocks rise far above you, with trees clinging to the extreme edge, as if peeping over to catch awful glimpses of the scene beneath. The water below the Fall is dark in color, except where it is lashed into little "white caps." The echo of the opposite cliff is almost stunning, deepening and more than doubling the roar of the Cataract, which doubtless from this regular and answering beat is called the "Triphammer Fall." It seems almost as if those "mills of the Gods" which "grind slowly" but "grind exceedingly small" might be turning their Cyclopean wheels inside the rocks. Above you is a narrow strip of calm and holy sky to relieve the somberness of the scene, and perhaps the sunshine is lighting up the Fall with sparkle and gleam and rainbow.

But alas! wretched mortal that I am. Here am I again trying to describe the indescribable, and to show off Nature's glories as if they were calico patterns. So I fly the scene, and leave you at the foot of "Triphammer," to find your way back through the Ravine till you discover a comfortable place to ascend to the heights above. Thence you move like an argosy richly freighted with golden memories to the place whence you set out, a wearier, but a wiser and I trust a better man. It will repay you to take the Sugar Loaf hill (which you will see on your right) by the way, for it commands one of the widest and loveliest prospects in all this region.

FALL CREEK,—SECOND FALL. ITHACA.

FALL CREEK.

A Southside View.

BY REV. F. N. ZABRISKIE.

TELL your hackman to drive you up the Dryden Road which passes the Cemetery gate. It is slow, up hill work to get out of Ithaca in almost any direction, but the tediousness is more than compensated by the unfolding landscape to which every step adds new breadth and beauty. After a half mile of panorama-seeing, you are greeted by the hoarse voice of Fall Creek, plunging and roaring, in its deep abyss. Your nature straightway chords itself up to a harmony with the wierd music, and you are ready for the wild and sublime scenes which lie before you. The road now runs parallel to the Ravine, and its romantic situation along the edge of the profound abyss, as also from its graceful windings and continuous shade, constitutes one of our most attractive drives. Pursue it for half a mile further or even a mile, but be sure to return to a point opposite the Dam. Here you dismiss your carriage to meet you near the Bridge at Fall Creek, and strike boldly into the woods, till you reach the Dam, which is no inconsiderable Fall in itself at high water; at least, it does very well to begin with, and enables you to moralize on the contrast between the waterworks of Art and of God. A good subject of comparison is just before you, in a Fall about the height of the Dam, but oh! how beautifully different from the smooth and graceful monotony of that. This little sidewise Fall, which turns its face to you as you start up the bank, flows across, and not down, the stream. On the left it plunges straight over, as if to show the Dam that it knows how to do that also. In the centre, the water breaks midway on a projection of rock, which splits and scatters it into a huge bouquet of foam flowers, while on the right several distinct cascades are thrown together into a narrow opening in the rocks with something of the result of mixing an inconceivably monstrous seidlitz powder. A deep, clear pool at its foot serves as a mirror for this gay and versatile young Fall to view her varied charms, of which she is so careful to present a front view to the visitor. You could say at first that she was an uncommonly noisy little coquette also, but although she has her full share of song, as well as beauty, and fleetness, you would do her injustice if you attributed all this racket to her alone, since the sound of two Falls are here blended remarkably into a duet.

If it be the afternoon of a bright day (which is always the fittest time for such an excursion), the opposite side will look very lovely and sunny, with its sloping bank covered with evergreens, and the soil brown and clean with their accumulated deposit of piny leaves. It looks peculiarly so, as you stand in the shadow and gaze across

FALL CREEK,—SIXTH FALL.

the wild flood. It may bring to mind consolingly, when our hearts are in the shade and chill of sorrow, the sunny land which lies beyond the whirl and tumult of this present life.

Proceed along the brink a short distance, and the other feature in this Duet of Floods lifting up their voices is discovered. You stand directly over "Triphammer Fall."* Its cyclopean hammers are ringing with the same steady and answering beat, and its solemn ravine is as impressive as when we viewed them from below. You will however notice better than before, how the water comes winding and gliding through its narrowing pass, till at the narrowest part of all it plunges over in an amber flood, and how just at the foot it strikes upon an opposing rock and rebounding breaks into the wildest foam. As you pass on do not be afraid of the brink. Most falls, unlike the "wee things" just described are coy and shrinking, and love, like Dryads, to hide behind thick veils of forest leaves. If you would catch her brightest glances, you must woo nature boldly, and pull aside the veil every now and then. After a succession of these "peeps," we come to nature's private box for viewing this exhibition, with the great advantage over private boxes in general of giving a front instead of a side view. It consists of a flat rock extending out over the ravine, and forming a natural platform, apparently hundreds of feet over the still dark stream. "Triphammer" may here be viewed in all its glory, and in the other direction the Ravine may be followed by the eye as far as Rocky Fall.

As you pass up the road (in fact all along the roadside),

---

*For a description of this and the other Falls mentioned in this sketch, see our former article on Fall Creek.

your attention is attracted by immense ant heaps. This seems to be a favorite residence for these industrious little citizens, for you will find a reference to these ant-hills in the account of a ramble along Fall Creek published no less than thirty years ago.

You leave the road again just beyond a huge railing formed of tree trunks, and dive into the woods for a distance of about twenty-five feet to the place where a gigantic elm towers, and its giant brother lies overthrown across your path. From this point you gain a remarkable view of no less than three (in fact, we may say, four), Falls; so brought into line juxtaposition, as to look like one continuous fall of at least two hundred feet. If it were indeed anything more than an optical illusion, it would be altogether the crowning Cataract of Ithaca.

A front view of the fourth or Rocky Fall may be obtained by leaving the road again when nearly opposite the barns which you presently approach. The descent is easy here to the bed of the stream, and a pleasant ramble will bring you immediately above the Fall, which may be viewed as closely and from as many points as was Triphammer just now. If you are not a very strong and resolute climber, however, you had better leave this out of your programme, as retracing your steps would prove so exhausting, as to unfit you perhaps for the remainder of the excursion.

For quite a distance now we can only take shuddering glimpses down the wooded sides of the precipitous ravine, and see only darkness or an occasional gleam of spray, and hear only a smothered roar as of dens of lions. At length we come to a place where a path diverges from the road before us, guarded at the entrance by an ancient and broken veteran of a tree. We descend, stooping under a fallen trunk, which lies across the path, and bids us "make our manners" on approaching one of nature's most sacred and lovely shrines. If you reach the Ravine at the farthest point on your right you obtain a fine view of Rocky Falls. If you keep straight along the ridge, you find yourself in a most secluded and favorite retreat of the writer, which he calls his "Eagle's Nest." You are on a rocky seat projecting out into the Glen. On three sides of you the rocks go hundreds of feet straight down; above your head there is an arbor of interlacing branches. The seat on which you sit, is luxuriantly cushioned with green moss two or three inches thick, that completely covers it, and the footstool below, with dry, warm soft upholstery. Opposite a frowning wall of rock, it rises from the bottom of the Glen, covered in winter ofttimes with shafts and stalactites of ice of the most enormous and imposing kind. There is, in fact, a grand and novel beauty about all these Ravines in the depth of winter, which one can scarcely realize in summer. As you sit in the sublime solitude of your "Eagles' Nest," you catch through the trees the gleam of Rocky Fall. Directly beneath your feet the voice of Foaming Fall rises tempting you with that peculiar sensation experienced on the brow of precipices, to cast yourself off, if perchance God's Angels will bear you up lest you dash your foot against a stone. To the left stretches away a picturesque and suggestive view second to none of which Ithaca can boast. You have a bird's eye view of the whole Glen below you and of the valley beyond. Come to this spot at about sunset of an Indian summer day, as I have done. The stream winding down in shadow between its rocky walls away out into the meadows and the Lake, the summits of the cliff all along the Ravine lighted up with the radiance of evening, the peaceful fields seen through the narrow portal at the farther end, the purple hills shutting in the horizon, the successive lines on the surface of the Creek which mark the plunge of Cataracts, the solemn warning voice of the floods, are all emblematic to the thoughtful mind, "What is your life?" they seem to say. It is even as a gliding stream, marked by critical situation over which it passes as down a steep, and closed in by high and narrow walls whose summits are touched with a glory that shineth from afar as from a setting sun, while through the narrow portals of the grave beyond, there lies a smiling country seen by the eye of faith and hope. Is it any wonder that I love this spot, whence the soul learns to mount up as on eagles' wings, or that I have given it the name just recorded?

On returning to the road another divergent footpath invites you, soon leading over a rail fence into a field. The path is now both pleasant and easy, the deep Ravine on one side and the broad landscape on the other. You are walking on an elevated plateau of land, and far below you are the village, the valley, and the Lake. There is however, but one favorable point along this whole path for viewing the Falls. The descent to this place is marked at present by some burnt and blackened logs. When you reach it, especially if the leaves are not too thick upon the trees, you have a striking glimpse of no less than three Falls.

By and by the edge of the Ravine becomes clearer of trees and the precipice more abrupt. As you stand on the brink you look directly down into the stream. Upon the opposite side the rocks stand out like some immense castle wall, with great buttresses and bastions and a deep dark moat at its foot. The path now descends rapidly, and in a moment or two you discern on the right a place where stones have been quarried to the very brink, leaving a lofty and conspicuous platform on the one side surmounted by a solitary Pine. This is directly above the Ithaca Fall, and commands a view also of the second or Forest Fall.

You next arrive at the entrance to the Tunnel. This is a Flume, excavated for a distance of a hundred feet through the solid rock. A body of water pours through sufficient to turn a dozen mills. Over this subterranean stream you walk on a platform of planks, and the cavernous gloom, the rushing water beneath, the stifled roar of the Falls beyond, and in Winter the long icicles that hang like stalactites from the ceiling, impart a novel and exciting sensation. On emerging at the farther end you stand in a scene of great grandeur and wildness, in view of the Forest Fall, and on the very brink of the Ithaca Fall, while above you tower the giant crags, and we descry many of the spots associated with our rambles on the margin of the Ravine. It is a good place too for trying the voice, just outside the Tunnel's mouth, which acts as a sounding board, and helps our feeble organs to cope with the thunder of the Fall and Dam. As you return be sure to step across the raging stream which tears like a demoniac down its craggy bed, upon the Rock Island formed by the Creek on one side, and the flume on three. Here Nature has provided a platform, with a tree or two to hold fast by, whence the finest view of Ithaca Fall is obtained. You are almost directly over it, and yet sufficiently, if front, to observe its whole surface.

You now seek the road through the yard of Andus McChain & Co's. paper mill. It will interest you however, even after all you have seen, to step aside and notice the course of the torrent which boils and roars and plunges down the narrow channel to the mills.

You bid farewell to Fall Creek on the Bridge, whence

you obtain the most picturesque view of the splendid Ithaca Fall. The screen of leaves behind which it seeks to hide its beauties, the Island in the centre of the stream, the romantic beauty of the upper Ravine, through which the water approaches the precipice, and the more quiet aspect of the descending sheet like a magnificent curtain dropped upon a series of panoramic views, leave a picture on your mind, which you gladly carry away as a memento of your afternoon's excursion.

TAGHKANIC FALLS

10 miles from Ithaca, 215 feet high.   Rocks on side of Ravine, 280 feet high.

TAGHKANIC FALLS.

BY WM. H. BOGART.

We settle and agree that this most beautiful of all the water descents of our State shall be designated TAGHKANIC. It is quite likely that we may not be entirely accurate in the orthography — and its syllables may in the common rendering be found out of place, but it is wisest to adopt what is so universal. A careful examination of its origin seems to indicate that it was called by the Indians "the Great Fall in the Woods," and as so remote, and shrouded in thick forest, and quite away from the Lake route of their canoes, the name seems appropriate. It is besides, euphonious, and we greatly prefer it to the designation of Goodwin's Falls, by which it was for many years known. The Goodwin family were respected settlers on or near to the extensive Point, which has been formed by the outpouring of soil for the ages, in the action of the little stream whose fall is the delight of all who see it. The name of the hamlet which forms the steamboat Landing is Goodwin's Point. It is about eight miles in a north-westerly direction from Ithaca. At the time these pages are written the access by the steamboat is easy, so far as the times and route of the boat is concerned, but the wharf is very insufficient — afforded to the traveler only by the courtesy of the owners of the paper mill which is Taghkanic's gift to the practical — the little pier is covered with a chaos of coal and merchandize, and is a very unsuitable entrance to a scene which is of the most interesting in all our State's book of nature. The proper facilities must yet be built, for every year will augment the number of the tourists who will be pilgrims to this chief cascade of all that circle Ithaca. A pier directly at the center of the Point, would give a fine road to the Falls, and would make a journey easier, which is quite enough surrounded with difficulty to make it interesting at all times. There are three ways of going to the Falls, or to the sight of them. We recommend all three of them, but to different classes. The young and active may easiest encounter difficulties which those less in possession of strength might best avoid, as very easily they can. There is a plain and good road all the way to Mr. Halsey's Hotel, which is beautifully placed on the bank that overlooks the Fall, and where can be found the neatness and order which makes it the pleasantest of all rural Hotels — with all that is convenient for a temporary home — with an excellent table — with all that is needed to enjoy the most leisurely view of Taghkanic. This road route is safely recommended as offering the least fatigue, and as accompanied by all that those who seek to clothe the hours with carpet could desire. Our eulogy of the Hotel is a genuine one. We repeat that it is the pleasantest of all that are in the surrounding of forest and field. But the view of the Falls from above is not that which enables Taghkanic to be seen as its beauty deserves. The next route is to pursue that plain and well marked road, keeping near the edge of the ravine, with care to the footstep 'till an entrance is seen to the long Staircase which admits a passage to the gorge below. This ladder of steps is a great convenience, and a safe one, to all of steady head. An invalid would find it a severe labor, but as they who visit Taghkanic are usually in the high glee of full strength and health, all the difficulties of the ascent and descent of these stairs are but in the catalogue of the events of the day. There is a defined path at the end of these steps — a sort of Indian trail tread, which can be easily followed, and it leads to the foot of the Fall.

But the best of all the ways in which the Taghkanic Fall is to be seen, and that which reveals all the glories of the great gorge, its beauty of varying forms, its wild grandeur, is *somewhat* to combine all the modes of access described. Soon after crossing the bridge near the Lake shore, there is a sudden and steep turn to the left, and a well worn path up a spur of a hill, the first chapter of *our* route. This hill is of the steepest climbing we are to encounter, and if successfully done, it may be regarded as something of the luxury of the worst being over. It is successfully done, and has been by the clever and the beautiful — by bright men and fair women, by all varieties of the adventurous, and its acclivity easily gained. Once at the top, the path skirts the ravine by the side of a cultured field, and gives as we pass, the superb view to the North of the CAYUGA, opening far and wide, its blue mirror fringed with all the gold of harvest in the gathering time — headland and bay blending their bold or curving lines in the long coast range. The land beyond Aurora is seen, and the picture fascinates to delay us before we find our path leading us downward, and the descent to the stream is made, over fallen trees, by ravine defile, and through tangled foliage till the water is reached. And here the adventurous visitor realizes the truth of the French maxim, ce n'est que le premier pas qui Coute. Our difficulty is in the beginning. Through a close network of young trees we find the creek intercepting our progress.

All the road up the gorge is wild and difficult, but

every step of it, is amidst scenery so picturesque that the toil is gladly borne. There is small use of bridge or foot path, for there are successive seasons in the year when the sudden fury of the water would remove the one and occupy the other, and thus at the first inevitable crossing of the creek, the way is left to the ingenuity of the tourist — to the strong arm and the ingenious hand. We *do* get over, and we will suppose that the transit is successfully made. It is only at this point that the creek need be crossed on the way up. The course is to keep to the left, and over a series of rough ways; through and along the gorge, we go around, a distance, about a mile — a vigorous mile of exertions to be abundantly rewarded at the close. All the journey up the ravine is a demand on our admiration, for the gorge is walled in by vast heights — of bare and of wooded rock. They rise treeless, and as if they would exhibit to us all the processes of geological condition, or so densely covered with forest, as that there seems a perpetual mystery in their concealment. Especially as we near the Fall, there is on the left hand, or south side, far and deep episodes of glen within the greater glen, leading off to invite us to explore them and detaining us from the onward progress. Few *do* make the exploration, and they abide summer and winter, nooks and recesses of woodland, the very chosen home of the Fawn and the Dryad, if the mystery of mythology were yet interlaced with *our* forest life. The bold heights are pinnacled and castellated, and the sky seems like a narrow river of blue ether flowing above us. We forget the rude roading in the study of this wildly written chapter of creation. We turn out of one of these deep wood paths to the right, and upon us is the Taghkanic — the most winning and beautiful of Falls. That pure veil of misty water, turning into woven air, almost from the instant it leaves the brow of the precipice, and so gently, so sweetly changing into foam — pure silver threaded wool like foam — and at last not dashing or breaking, but gliding into the chasm below. There are what seem, different fibres, (if we may use that word), of the water that make up the Fall and these are intermingled in sweetness of union. The water has a descent so free that it seems to use a leisure of movement, and it is easy to enumerate the seconds in the time of the fall. Beneath it nearly all the way, the rock is visible, and there is a foliage there that is thus perpetually bathed by the crystal cascade. It is a very diamond of beauty, set in all the rugged and fierce scenery of that dark and wild glen. It is like a fairy surrounded by a rude guard of giants. It is a surprise of loveliness amidst darkness and gloom. The glen has intended to give a great amphitheatre for the Fall, which true to its shy sweetness of notice, occupies but brief space in that extended circle. A little pool seems to be in constant attendance at the foot of the cascade, as if lingering to talk to the Taghkanic, before it should tell the story of its far leap, to the Cayuga, to which it is to hasten. Great mounds of debris are beneath the cliffs, and boulders are scattered in profusion, welcome seats and convenient tables to those who are fascinated to linger here. Our friends who have taken the easier upper route are perhaps signaling us from above, but they are so far beyond us, that we but imperfectly see them, and indeed with better taste than to look at any humanity, we are gazing at the TAGHKANIC itself, seeking to imprint its memories so truthfully that there shall be something of vivid reality in the delineation which we shall utter with so much fervor to those who have not yet seen this loveliness.

The first emotion on seeing this Fall from below, is

one of surprise — not at its height, for we lose the details of the 215 feet of perpendicular, unbroken descent, in the greater effects, but at its pleasant character — we looked for something to rage and roar in its fearful plunge. It is not that which Taghkanic delineates for us in its picture. It comes to us — it moves to us — it rather floats down and seems as if something of peace and tenderness was its accompaniment. Heralded to us by all the genii of the gorge and the glen, out of dark and deep wood and fell forest, it has its own distinct calm, as if it would soothe and soften us after our weary and wild walk. The gentle Taghkanic claims its own peculiar beauty. It lives in this rough ravine, as if it were the very guardian angel of all the scene, and had only a look and language of kindness, whatever might be the frown around it of all this shadowed glen. We turn from it with the regret with which we leave a scene to which in our conscience and taste we know the best within us has made fellowship. We shall remember this when the cares of life have crowded around us again, and this soothing water shall flow over our hearts in ever pleasant remembrance.

Few return the entire length of the glen, and we do not recommend this. It is wisest to take the left hand path and seek the stairs, which, once ascended, we are prepared to find, just what we do find in Mr. HALSEY's house, a delightful rest, and a delicious refreshment. These stairs *are* formidable, but if taken, as we should take life's troubles, cool and easy and one at a time, they are but a pleasant incident in the adventures of the day, and indeed they so diversify the route, that it is a succession of novel enterprises.

If the inanimate can feel emotion, our Lake Country may well be proud of its TAGHKANIC. It has no rival — no superior. It does not belong to the family of the stern and savage Trenton, so resistless and impetuous; but it *does* place itself at the very head of all the beautiful in the cascades of this State. Most fortunately all its surroundings are as we could desire. The glen is just as rude and wild as the charm of contrast could require. The Lake forms the most delightful road thither. It is not too remote from — not too near to — the great highway. It has its own most agreeable Hotel, and Ithaca with all its incidents of a busy life, is within an easy sail or drive — and thus in our delineation of the Scenery around the Village of The UNIVERSITY — we must assign the first place in the attractions of its neighborhood to the TAGHKANIC.

LUCIFER FALLS.

BY WM. H. BREWER.

Among the many picturesque spots near Ithaca, none better repay a visit, nor leave a more pleasing impression than Enfield Falls. The town in which they occur, and which gives them their name, is a fine agricultural region, and fertile farms crown its rich swelling slopes, which are dotted with woodlands, portions of the virgin forest that covered all these hills but a generation since. The writer was reared among these hills, about two miles from the falls, and like many other boys of the neighborhood, was familiar with the spot, long before it became known to the world outside. A Grist Mill stood near the entrance of the ravine. Here the family flour was ground, and often, long years ago, while "waiting for a grist," with other boys, we penetrated the mysterious but fascinating "Gulf." That was what *we* called it.

To be sure, a party of tourists from a distant city had visited it about this time, and had called it Lucifer Falls, and had given fanciful names to various portions of the ravine, but to us, it was simply, The Gulf.

In those times it was of difficult access, and a visit was attended with much fatigue, and not a little danger; but these only made a visit more to be desired by adventurous boys. We crawled along narrow shelves of rock, sometimes could only reach lower levels by climbing into the tops of trees and descending their trunks.

RAVINE ABOVE LUCIFER FALLS.

We ventured across slippery, slimy rocks; but the risk was amply rewarded if we could only get to the top of the Main Fall, look over its crest, and see the foaming flood go tumbling, tumultuous into the abyss below, watch the spray rise, and listen to the hollow roar that came back from the nether deep. If the water was high, this point could not be reached, then we would stop in the narrower part of the gorge, and screech and yell to awaken the echoes of the place. Mysterious stories were current, how bears still lurked there, how rattlesnakes watched for intruders, and how counterfeiters had their shops and had built forges, and carried on their dark work in this wild spot, where few men would venture!

We were never rewarded with a sight of any of these, yet a firm belief in their existence, was only shaken by increasing years.

To get below the Falls was an undertaking of less risk but more labor. We had to descend the steep bank from the very top, some distance below. Nevertheless we accomplished it nearly every summer, and it was a hard day's work. Great was the delight when we got into this chasm, and looked up and saw the foaming waters coming from so far above. A swim in the clear, deep pool at the base of the Fall was one of the rewards of the labor. But delightful as these trips were to "us boys," they had often to be undertaken clandestinely. Parents could not see it in the same light, for aside from the risk to life and limb, we generally returned with clothes wet and torn, and with bruised limbs.

In later years we have seen many other scenes of natural beauty, have wandered among the Alps, seen the beauty of Tyrol, the wonders of Yosemite, and the grandeur of Niagara; yet Enfield Falls seem no less beautiful than they did in those youthful days, and a visit to the old home would not be complete without seeing them.

Far different is a visit now, from what I have described. There is no danger, no discomfort, and but little fatigue, thanks to the enterprise and taste of the owner.

The place is about six miles south-west of Ithaca, and the ride is a charming one. We first pass up the fertile valley of the Inlet for two or three miles, luxuriant crops of rustling corn, or rank tobacco, stretch across the valley in great fields. The sluggish stream winds through it by many a crook and turn, with its banks fringed with sycamores and willows. On either side, high but gentle hills shut out the distant view.

And now we begin to ascend the West Hill. It is a long but gentle slope, and the beauties increase as we rise. Wider and wider becomes the field of view as hill beyond hill comes in sight. The valley we have left is spread out before us like a map. The pretty village of Ithaca lies nestled among the trees. The hills beyond seem tilted up as if for our inspection, every farm and woodland, and road, and ravine is in distinct view, and off at the north, the Lake adds its charms to the scene. But the finest view is towards the south. In this direction lies a rougher country. We see far up the valley we have left; hill rises beyond hill, each higher than the one before, to the great ridge which divides the waters flowing north into Lake Ontario, and south into the Chesapeake. This ridge forms the distant blue horizon. Fertile farms spot the rolling hills, the woodlands forming a larger element in the landscape as it becomes more distant.

This view is always one of surpassing beauty, whether seen in the lively green of spring, or in the heat of sum-

ENFIELD FALL,—MAIN FALL, SIX MILES FROM ITHACA.

From Photograph by J. C. Burritt.

mer, when the ripe grain waiting for the harvest contrasts its rich hues with the dark green forests, or in autumn when the woods have put on their gorgeous colors, and when the shadows of more frequent clouds chase each other over the landscape, the first precursors of winter.

Before we are aware of it, or have viewed this charming picture to our satisfaction, we turn a corner, a little valley lies ahead of us into which we descend, and are at the Enfield Mills near the Falls. We stop at Enfield Falls' Hotel, where our horses will be cared for, and our own wants attended to. Mrs. W., the worthy hostess of the house, is the proprietress of the land upon which the Falls and Ravine are, and whose care keeps the paths and bridges in repair, for the accommodation of the public. Here we leave our horses, order our dinner, and then set out on foot.

A few rods walk brings us to the mouth of the ravine, where we cross the stream. Before entering, we turn and look back. The valley widens out above, pastures cover the slopes, a cluster of houses and gardens are in the bottom, among which the large flouring mill looms up like the father of the flock. The hills close in where we are, as if to bar the progress of the stream. And this they doubtless once did, forming a lake above. Terraces on both sides of the valley, at nearly the same height, indicate this, and other facts appear to confirm it. This lake must have been drained by the stream cutting the ravine which we will now enter.

The beauties begin at the very threshold. The rock is of soft slates and shales, alternating with strata of harder sandstones, all lying nearly horizontal. The softer shales wear away, and the harder sandstones form numerous cascades, and also forms the bed of the ravine, which in places is nearly as level as a floor. The strata fracture in straight lines, and thus are formed walls and buttresses, marvelously regular, and adorned with frieze and cornice and battlement as if crazy architects had mingled half a dozen styles. Steps, and walls, and terraces are there. The narrow places have been widened by art, and the way is easy and pleasant.

We pass down on the right side of the stream, which falls over its rocky bed in frequent cascades. At the foot of the first of these there are several remarkable "pot holes" worn by the action of the water in the rock. One of these is as regular and nearly as round as a well, its sides perpendicular and polished. It is filled with clear green water, and the little cascade falls into one side of it. Others are less regular; but all have curved sides beautifully polished, and some of them are very deep. The stream narrows and soon rushes for some distance in a narrow channel, like a plume, a mere trough in the smooth rock. Here we cross it by a neat bridge about twenty feet above the rushing water. The ravine grows deeper and wider as we follow down the stream, the sides sometimes rising in walls, at others, the rock is weathered and covered with trees and bushes.

We now descend a rude rocky staircase into what was formerly called "The Devil's Kitchen." It is a sort of recess on one side, with marvelously regular walls, and a rocky floor, both of which have lost some of their smoothness by crumbling during the last twenty years. There we have more narrow rocky shelves to pass along, and more steps to descend and new beauties to see at each turn, when we reach the head of the Main Fall.

Not the least striking feature in the scene is the aspect of the vegetation. Hemlocks, cedars, pines and other trees cling to the steep side where there is soil to nou-

RAVINE,—LUCIFER FALLS.

From Photograh by J. C. Burritt.

rish them, or crevices for their roots to hold their roots. Rock Maple with its delicate tassels of flowers, Yew, with its amber-like berries, grow from the crevices. Graceful ferns droop from the rocks, and wild vines festoon them, delicate mosses and curious lichens adorn the gnarled roots, or carpet the rocks. The delicate Hare-bell nods here and there, and the grass of Parnassus, with its exquisite white flowers blooms on the slimy rocks, and the scientific botanist finds here many other rare and curious plants, seldom seen by the common observer, to gladden his eye and enrich his herbarium.

The main fall is not perpendicular, but the water goes tumbling and rebounding down the rocks in masses of foam. Its height is said to be 160 feet, (or I should say its *depth*, for we see it first from above), the sides of the ravine rising nearly a hundred feet higher. We can stand at the very brink of the fall and see the waters go bounding away in spray and foam into the deep abyss below us. Here the scene changes.

In the part of the Ravine we have passed through, we are most deeply impressed by the picturesque beauty; but here is grandeur. Above the Falls the scenes are pretty,— below they are sublime.

A well-made and safe path permits an easy descent to their base. We first pass down some steps close by the splashing water for a short distance, and then on a shelf cut along the face of the rock, getting grand views at each turn. Now we pass along the narrow shelf with high precipices towering overhead, and descending deep beneath. And then by a bridge built against the rocky wall, from which we look down into the dizzy depth. This part of the path is but short. We now leave the rock, and pass down a winding way among the trees to the bottom.

Here one sees the Falls from below, and they seem bigger from our change of position. The walls seem higher and the precipices grander as we see them from this point, with their upper edge thrusting its sharp outlines high up against the clear sky.

Below this the Ravine widens out and becomes less abrupt. It has many quiet scenes of picturesque beauty that would delight the artist; but it seems tame after visiting the wild portion we have passed, so we will not pass down it, but will retrace our steps.

As we pass back, we will all notice many beauties that escaped us on our way down, and perhaps no two of our party will agree as to which is the finest view. We will notice some things more in detail, and perhaps near the "kitchen," some of the party will point out the curious hollows in the rocky floor. Many of these resemble tracks made by huge moccasined feet, and our poet, if he chance to be along, can easily tell stories of gigantic hunters, Titans in size, who left their tracks here when the rock was softer in the earlier ages of the world.

The prosier part of our party, however, will account for them by the action of water. Then with spirits exhilarated by the scenes, and appetites sharpened by the pure air and the exercise, all will hasten back to the ample dinner prepared by the worthy hostess of the Enfield Falls' Hotel.

LUCIFER FALLS AND RAVINE.

"To sit on rocks, to muse o'er flood and fell,
To slowly trace the forest's shady scene,
Where things that own not man's dominion dwell,
And mortal foot hath ne'er, or rarely been;
To climb the trackless mountain all unseen,
With the wild flock that never needs a fold:
Alone o'er steeps and foaming falls to lean:
This is not solitude; 'tis but to hold
Converse with Nature's charms, and view her stores unrolled."

MONG the many places of interest with which a bountiful Nature has supplied this favored locality, perhaps there is no one point more acceptable to the appreciative tourist, than the magnificent Cataract upon "Five Mile" Creek, known as "Lucifer Falls;" a name which savors of so great antiquity, that it is not probable a bard can now be found among the many who inhabit the adjacent hills, whose heroic harp continues to echo the reasons of its giving.

Although there are many cascades of great beauty — deep mysterious gorges — tremendous barriers of rock, and grand forest solitudes to be encountered at every turn of the path which conducts the visitor along the course of this picturesque stream, yet, for a rare combination of all that is thought excellent in wild landscape scenery, the grand descent of " Lucifer" stands preëminently alone, and is the point to be sought by the tourist who is so fortunate as to be wandering in its vicinity.

About a half mile above the Fall, the little creek, which has its rise among the blue hills beyond, suddenly enters a narrow but formidable gateway of rock, whose huge buttresses tower a hundred feet above on either side, surmounted with a bristling growth of hemlock and pine. The course of the stream having been comparatively free from obstruction until now, winding through a beautifully formed valley of green pastures and meadow land, where many an honest tiller of the soil has erected his comfortable home, now becomes painfully tortuous, broken with sharp angles, and obstructed with fragments of rock which have fallen from the heights above; and the water which has idly found its way thus far, prepares in earnest for the desperate encounter which seems inevitable, and plunges into the shadows of the gorge as if curious to explore its mysteries, and strong to endure the torment which it may inflict.

Probably there is no Ravine in the world which furnishes more variety in so short a space, as that which extends from the rocky entrance so securely guarded by the two granite Champions, to the dizzy verge of the grand fall a few hundred yards below. Every foot of progress discloses some new and singular formation of rock entirely dissimilar from any preceding it. Cascades of every conceivable form and height, and deep, narrow channels which sometimes conceal in their rumbling depths the fiercely running water, follow each other in such rapid and agreeable succession, that the spectator is at once lost in wonder and delight. Throughout the entire course, a safe and easy foot path winds along be-

LUCIFER FALLS.—MAIN FALL.

neath the overhanging cliffs, and at a point about midway from the entrance crosses the gulf, thirty feet above the water, by a rustic bridge, from which a grand view of the Ravine is obtained, both up and down the stream.

So picturesque, and at times sublime, is the scenery on either hand, that the tourist, as he descends, sometimes forgets that he has not yet beheld the grand object of his visit, and shudders with astonishment when at length, upon turning an abrupt corner of the cliff, the fearful gulf, whose rocky pavement checked the rash leap of "Lucifer," stares him in the face!

> "The roar of waters! from the headlong height
> Velino cleaves the wave-worn precipice;
> The fall of waters! rapid as the light
> The flashing mass forms, shaking the abyss;
> The hell of waters! where they howl and hiss,
> And boil in endless torture; while the sweat
> Of their great agony, wrung out from this
> Their Phlegethon, curls round the rocks of jet
> That gird the gulf around, in pitiless horror set."

Two hundred and twenty feet beneath, the water, already recovered from the concussion of the fall, is seen dimly through the mist-wreaths to flow leisurely along, and disappear in the shadow of green foliage beyond. One hundred and fifty feet above, are buried the roots of trees which crown the noble brow of the cliff, and thrust still another hundred feet into the sunlight of heaven, wave the top-most boughs, which sway fearlessly over an abyss of nearly five hundred feet in depth!

After the first thrill of admiration inspired by this unsurpassed scene has passed away, the visitor will, without longer delay, avail himself of the stairway that has been built for the purpose, and descending to the rocky platform below, follow the spiral path along the side of the precipice, which will soon conduct him to the bottom of the Ravine, about a hundred yards below the Fall, the dashing music of which is constantly heard sweeping around the angles of the cliff. Now, after making a short turn to the right, a few steps of progress discloses the best general view of the Fall, and is the point where the drawing was made which illustrates this sketch. When the afternoon sun in summer looks down over the western cliff, gilding with glory the extended boughs of the old hemlocks, and lights up the sparkling moss and flashing water — when the deep, pure blue of the upper heaven is spread in holy majesty above, and no sight nor sound of human passion disturbs the dread, yet beautiful solemnity of the scene — then should the pilgrim of Nature seek the romantic glen of Lucifer, and worship for an hour at her majestic shrine.

PULPIT FALL, BUTTERMILK CREEK, ITHACA.

From a Photograph by J. C. Burritt.

BUTTERMILK FALLS.

These falls are the most accessible of all those that surround Ithaca, with the exception of Fall Creek, and for picturesque beauty are unequaled.

The usual, and, in fact, the only route by which they are reached, is by what is called the Newfield road, beginning at the foot of Cayuga street, and running through the beautiful valley of Newfield to the town of that name.

The road is good either for riding or driving, and from its gradual ascent presents a fine view of Ithaca and the Lake.

Shortly after leaving town the road passes through a singular cut in the hills, that is continued up and down many hundred yards, and forming a cut or grade that is very conspicuous from the village. This "Inclined Plane," as it is called, was once the substitute for the seemingly tedious curves and switches by which the present rail road reaches the level of the valley; but several serious accidents induced the directors to adopt the longer but safer method.

The ride to the Falls is most charming; the rise in the road is slight, and the hills along whose base it runs shelter it from the winds and sun.

Nearly two miles from town the road passes under the track of the rail road, and, making an abrupt turn, brings the tourist face to face with the

I.

FIRST FALL.

The hill, before unbroken, is here cleft by a mountain torrent, that comes pouring over the sharp rocks of its bed in a mass of thick, frothy foam, that evidently suggested to the unæsthetic and domestic countryman the name of

BUTTERMILK FALLS.

The view is indeed superb; the perpendicular sides of the chasm crowned with "dark'ning pines," forming a fit frame for the falls of dazzling purity, the ruins of the quaint old saw-mill at their base, and above the first fall, around a seeming curve, half hidden by the sombre forest, seen through mossy pines and hemlocks, is the second fall, crowning the first with a chaplet of spotless white, and falling silently in a mass of feathery foam.

The tourist can never tire of standing at the foot of the first fall, soothed by the soft whispers of the foamy stream, and charmed by the vivid contrasts of color in the dull, grey ravine, the brilliant, sunny cascade, and, over all, the blue of the sky.

It is hard to convince one that these two beautiful falls are but the beginning of a series of cascades, less in size but equal in beauty, and that the ascent is practicable as well for ladies and children as for the stronger members of the party.

THE ASCENT.

There are two methods of reaching the level of the stream above; one, in comparatively dry seasons, by ascending directly the bed of the stream; and the other, when that is overflowed, by the west bank.

Either of these two routes will conduct the visitor to

the summit of the ravine, and both are quite easy. The one by the bed of the stream is most used, and we will suppose that the one taken, with an occasional reference to the other.

The bed of the first fall is so inclined that it presents a series of small steps that break up the stream into a mass of foam, and afford an easy method of ascent.

Mounting some one hundred and twenty-five or fifty feet, we reach the level platform at the top of the first fall, and pausing in our ascent look back.

Standing just midway between the two falls, at the summit of the first and the foot of the second, we look down on the tossing, boiling waters, torn into foamy fragments by the pointed rocks, and sliding over, step after step, until it reaches the quiet level of the valley.

The chasm still rises above us, sombre in its neutral tint, here and there marked by lichens and a few trailing vines that are nourished by the moisture from the falls. The Valley of Ithaca lies open below us with a dreary expanse of marsh, beyond it the spires of the churches glistening in the sunlight; the far off hills with irregular patches of green or ripening grain, in vivid verdancy or matured gold! The deep blue lake beyond all, hemmed in by the hills, tossing and breaking into snow capped waves or glassy in its perfect quiet. The view is only equaled by the one from the summit of the fall above us.

We clamber on, our eye arrested every moment by some new beauty in the eddying waters or in the mossy woods and trailing vines that festoon the trees.

The bed of the

SECOND FALL

is more perpendicular than the first, and we find the steps a little wider apart, and the water comes down more rapidly and full of noise, murmuring and sighing at leaving the cool, calm stream above to be tossed and torn by succeeding falls. Reminding one of Southey's lines:

> ——— "And dashing and flashing, and splashing and clashing,
> And so never ending but always descending,
> Sounds and motions for ever and ever are blending
> All at once and all o'er with a mighty uproar,
> And this way the water comes down at Lodore."

We glance from the noisy stream to the silent woods with their profusion of velvety moss that covers in its kindliness the decayed trunks of the fallen trees, as the birds buried beneath a tomb of leaves the "children in the wood."

The second Fall being only about one hundred feet high, we soon reach the second plateau and our climbing is nearly over.

The chasm widens out, its sides seem to rise still higher, and we stand in an immense amphitheatre and in front of us is the celebrated

PULPIT ROCK.

From the summit of the second Fall, one has a still more extensive view of the valley and the lake beyond, with glimpses through the trees of sunny hills and quiet farms of the village beyond the woods, silent in the purple haze of fall or Indian summer, or seeming to tremble in the undulating quivering atmosphere of midsummer. With a lingering glance towards the hills with all their grades and contrasts of color, we turn to the remarkable scene before us.

The amphitheatre of which we have spoken as formed by the widening of the Ravine, closes gradually around in our front, and is there broken by a narrow cleft extending down to within thirty feet of the level on which we stand. There the rocks project in a semicircular

PULPIT FALL ON BUTTERMILK CREEK.

form, making the most perfect "pulpit" or "stand" conceivable. Other places have claimed that name for a paltry rock or two standing on each other, or a slight projection from the face of a cliff; but here is a pulpit built by the hands of the Great Orator, and uttering, as loudly as temples fashioned by hands, His truths.

The pulpit proper is about forty feet wide and thirty high, gradually rounding out at the sides and perpendicular. The narrow gorge that ends in it, makes a sudden turn some yards back, and leaves, or seems to leave, a niche in the rocks a yard or two in width, in which one expects to see the occupant of that rocky pulpit installed and chaunting to the sound of the murmuring waters the praises of Him of whom we read,

> "The groves were God's first temples, ere man learned
> To hew the shaft and lay the Architrave,
> And spread the roof above them,— ere he framed
> The lofty vault to gather and roll back
> The sound of anthems: in the darkling wood.
> Amidst the cool and silence, he knelt down,
> And offered to the Mightiest, solemn thanks
> And supplication."

The sides of the Ravine frown down on the tourist and shut out the cheerful sun, and all is silence save the trickling of the little stream that falls over the pulpit rock.

In dry weather when the stream is very low the rock is almost dry and can be surmounted from its base; but the better way, particularly if there are any ladies in the party, is to make a detour in the woods, (on the right hand bank) and reach the stream by clambering down its banks some thirty or forty rods above pulpit rock and then walk down to it. Unless the rocks be wet the descent from the bank is easy and perfectly safe. We will suppose the visitor has reached in this or the other way, Pulpit rock.

In front is the huge amphitheatre and the sharp line of foam that marks the summit of the second cascade, and we have a faint glimpse of the distant valley bounded by the range of blue hills.

We are standing some thirty feet above the platform we have just left and ten or fifteen feet in front or projecting from the ravine to which the pulpit rock is attached. The narrow gorge through which the stream winds, turns so abruptly that we think the channel must be lost in some charmed fountain, or have disappeared in some mysterious subterranean water course. Over head the sides of the ravine nearly touch and the hemlocks mingle their dark branches. We walk onward and find that the gorge widens as it comes down and its sides are hollowed out in strange forms by the action of the water. The channel of the stream is but a few feet wide and has worn a cut in the rocks through which the water rushes, eddying and turning in a thin line. Just where the gorge turns at almost right angle we see a curious effect of the action of the water on the rocks. A stone is whirled over a smooth space and gradually wears a hollow; the process continues for years, and the result at last is a perfectly circular well worn in the rock here twelve feet in diameter and some nine feet deep, forming a very appropriate churn from whence the buttermilk flows, or presenting to a more imaginative mind a Bath in which the attendant nymphs of the woods might disport during the long hot hours of the summer. Just beyond this bath the channel comes falling down some ten or twelve feet, and above that fall is another curious well of an oblong cresent shape. Beyond this another slight fall, then a half well. The gorge is still narrow and in the summer by the exclusion of the sun deliciously cool. One longs to rest forever stretched on the rocks, and lulled by the soft murmur of the water, to rest and dream, and the sweet song of the

"Mild eyed, melancholy Lotus sated"

floats through one's memory with its cadence soft as the plashing waters.

> "There is sweet music here that softer falls
> Than petals from blown roses on the grass,
> Or night dews on still waters between walls
> Of shadowy granite, in a gleaming pass ;
> Music that gentlier on the spirit lies
> Than tired eye-lids upon tired eyes,
> Music that brings sweet sleep down from the blissful skies.
> There are cool mosses deep,
> And through the moss the ivies creep,
> And in the stream the long-leaved flowers weep
> And from the craggy edge the poppy hangs in sleep,
> ......How sweet it were hearing the downward stream
> With half shut eyes, ever to seem
> Falling asleep in a half dream !
> ......To muse and brood and live again in memory
> With those old faces of our infancy
> Heaped over with a mound of grass,
> Two handfuls of white dust shut in an urn of brass !"

There are several more of these curious walls or paths, and the series ends in a small one some five or six feet in diameter, at the foot of a narrow channel cut deep in the rock, rising some ten or twelve feet, and not more than two wide, through which the whole stream is forced, and glides with intense rapidity in a smooth, dark coil of water.

The tourist can continue in the glen from pulpit rock through its entire length, and can not fail to admire the smooth, clear rocks, polished and worn by the waters. Ascending in convenient steps the banks, some twenty or thirty feet high, composed of horizontal strata of rocks covered with lichens, brown, white and every shade of grey, fringed with trailing vines and curious vivid moss.

From the narrow channel or flume just mentioned, glancing up the stream a most beautiful view is presented. The stream flows on between straight, narrow banks, arched over by trees, forming a shady vista, and one above the other; rising higher in the distance, are four well defined cascades, the water falling in sheets of foam and contrasting strongly with the dark green of the trees and the neutral tint of the banks. These cascades are, respectively, ten, twenty, ten and twelve feet high. We can not dwell on this beautiful view; the cascades rising one above the other with a gleam of sunlight sometimes falling through the trees and reflecting back in dazzling rays the soft sound of the water; the lichened bank and moss grown trees combine to form a scene that, for picturesque beauty, is seldom equaled in this country.

When we reach the fourth fall of the series just mentioned, the character of the scenery changes, and the banks, losing their rocky steepness, slope gradually down to the water's edge. The stream glides along with but few interruptions of cascades in its easy descent, and the trees are reflected back in its smooth surface in all their perfection of form and color. We have gone a little more than one half of the whole extent of the stream, and our attention being continually attracted by some new beauty in the stream or wood, we can hardly believe we have gone so far.

The stream grows more and more brook-like, and murmuring over its rocky bed seems gleefully singing:

> "I chatter over stony ways
>   In little sharps and trebles,
> I bubble into eddying bays,
>   I babble on the pebbles.
>
> I wind about, and in and out,
>   With here a blossom sailing,
> And here and there a lusty trout,
>   And here and there a grayling.
>
> And here and there a foamy flake
>   Upon me as I travel,
> With many a silv'ry water break,
>   Above the golden gravel."

We pause and notice the exquisite ferns that fringe the rocks, and spring up in tufts on the fallen trees that the moss has nearly covered. The woods are evergreen, and we have visited them in winter when only the silent, ice-bound stream altered the scene from that of the past summer; the woods were the same, the moss as profuse and soft. The scene is one of intense quiet and peace.

> —— "The mossy rocks themselves,
> And the old and ponderous trunks of prostrate trees
> That lead from knoll to knoll a causeway wide,
> Or bridge the sunken brook, and their dark roots,
> With all their earth upon them, twisting high,
> Breathe fixed tranquility. The rivulet
> Sends forth glad sounds, and, tripping o'er its bed
> Of pebbly sands or leaping down the rocks,
> Seems with continuous laughter to rejoice
> In its own being."

The brook-like stream has been quiet too long, and, lest its character should be lost, makes an abrupt bend and presents a view only second to the one that meets us on surmounting the second grand fall. The banks have gradually risen until they again tower a hundred or two feet above us, their sides bare and sombre and their bases nearly meeting; the stream has widened to some fifty feet, and falls in a cascade of rare beauty some twenty or thirty feet, its width seemingly lessened by the projecting banks, and we catch a glimpse of the stream widening out, behind their dark edges. Just above the cascade, and in towards the bank, in bold relief against the dark rocks, rises a mass of stone, a pillar fringed with moss and ferns, rearing itself straight up fifty feet and tapering to a point crowned with vines and flowers.

This extraordinary rock is called indiscriminately Steeple Rock, Chimney Rock, and

MONUMENT ROCK.

The latter name seems to us the most appropriate, for looking up to it from the lower glen, it stands there solitary in its beauty and symmetry: like a funeral obelisk pointing its finger to the sky, a fit monument and reminder of the generations who have passed away, while *its* only change has been a little more added ferns and moss, and a little wearing away by the water!

Climbing cautiously around the right hand bank of the stream on a ledge seemingly cut out for the convenience of the tourist, and rounding the projecting bank, we come in full view of the cascade, above which rises the Monument Rock. Part of the cascade falls through a cleft in the rock, and the crushed water rising in a cloud of spray reflects back the sunlight in a beautiful rainbow, the dark rock rises near it and adds another charm to a scene picturesque beyond description.

Standing on the right-hand bank and glancing across the stream, the tourist will be struck by the singular carcase appearance of the bank, the water has worn away the softer more friable part of the bank, leaving a sharp point that hems in the stream. We strongly advise the visitor to climb the bank and reach the projection that corresponds with the one just noticed, he will then be standing above Monument Rock with its ferns and lichens, its vines and flowers. It rises, measured from the stream, fifty feet or more; the strata of rock that compose it, project over each other so as to form a circular pathway to its summit, which has been reached by expert climbers.

With a lingering glance back at the wonderful rock we continue our onward course. There remains but little to mention now, the stream winds through narrow rocky banks, the one side steep, grey, ragged and sombre in color; the other sloping and wooded. There is but one cascade of any size above Monument Rock. The banks on the north side lower a little, and before us are the ruins of an old saw mill carried away in a recent freshet, and a rude bridge crossing the stream, which marks the end of Buttermilk Ravine.

Beyond this point the stream winds through green fields and gentle slopes, and is lost in the hills further south.

A road to Ithaca crosses the stream on the bridge mentioned above, and the walk from this point to town, affords one of the finest views of Ithaca and the lake that can be obtained.

Parties visiting the Falls can drive in their carriages to the first Fall, and have the carriage driven around to the upper bridge and await them there.

Three hours can be easily and pleasantly passed in the Ravine, and the distance from the bridge to town by the upper road is not quite three miles, a delightful walk in the cool of the evening, during the sunsets for which Ithaca is so famous.

NOTE.—We have supposed the tourist to visit the Falls during summer or fall; but we have found them accessible and beautiful beyond description even in winter, by keeping on the south or right-hand bank, and not descending into the Ravine. The ice bound stream, the motionless cascades, fixed silent in all beautiful forms, the banks hung with immense icicles, and stranger than all, the remarkable vernal appearance of the woods, render such a visit well worth the increased trouble.

LICK BROOK.

Where is Lick Brook? How do you go to Lick Brook? Who discovered Lick Brook? These were the questions that were frequently asked in the summer of the Year of Grace, 1864. It came out conversationally, that a few people had been there, in the early summer of that year. Upon being questioned,— It was a "Wonderful place." "It was Beautiful." It was a "Fearful place." "You must go there." "Don't think of going." "You never can get there." "Do go by all means." These, and similar, were the answers. They were very indefinite, but very well calculated to heighten the questioner's curiosity.

A party started one warm summer morning, to go to Lick Brook. They were provided with baskets and a

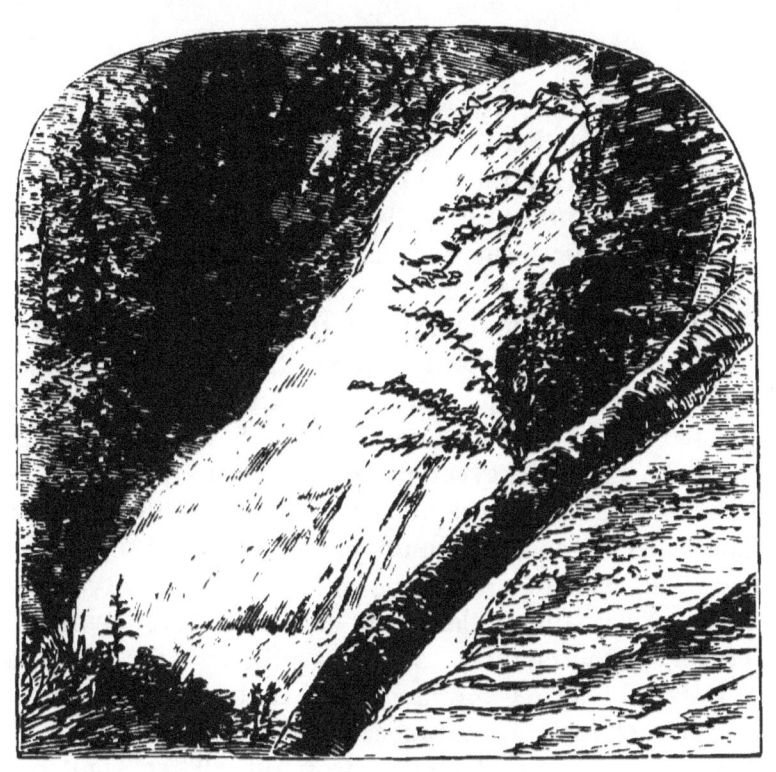

LICK BROOK, FIRST FALL, ITHACA.

From Photograph by J. C. Burritt.

bottle, and it being ascertained also, that one of the party carried a pistol, it was declared safe to proceed.

They started on the road, known in the vernacular as, " the way to Buttermilk Falls." Do you know the way? No! You have been there? No!! Has any one of us been there? No!!!

Following the highway, up the valley, for perhaps three quarters of an hour, and meeting with no greater danger than a passing rail road train, (ladies are never alarmed at sight of a train of cars; oh no!) they were suddenly and with great presence of mind, stopped in the vicinity of a farm house, and one of the number dispatched to scour the country, and collect information. The result was, to open the nearest and most convenient gate, and turn into a lane. It does not seem to be the custom of the country to ask permission of a man to drive into his fields and lanes; but if the astonished proprietor makes his appearance, to shout, "Is this the way to Lick Brook?" and apply the whip. They went on. The stream ran over the road, and the road ran through the stream. They clasped their hands, looked despairingly in one another's faces, and safely forded; found themselves in a marsh, in a thicket, and then in the stream. They flanked a tree, and went ingloriously around a stump, and over a log, and crossed the stream several times more, and being now accustomed to danger, never discovered that the horses were running away. One was speculating on the chances of petroleum, the indications being an oily, green substance on the little pools of water; and another, on the probable value of the crops raised, and the fine opportunity for investing in real estate, and water privileges. The horses were sensible animals, however, and finally yielded to a judicious amount of bit, and brake, and rather forcible persuasion. The road, what there was of it, now giving signs of discontinuing, they hailed a landsman, an "original settler" probably, for he was felling a tree, were advised to stop soon and try a different kind of locomotion. The horses were therefore tied up, and the baskets and valuables left to their keeping, a sarcastic individual quoting an Arab proverb. "They are safe; give yourself no uneasiness, O Effendi; there is not a Christian in the country."

They next climbed a fence. There are things more easy of accomplishment than to get a large party over a fence, and while they were engaged in falling over it, getting caught in it, anathemizing it, one of the party, (who carried a fishing pole and a private bottle), was accidentally lost. All efforts to find him were vain, and the party were reluctantly compelled to go on without him. They were now breast high in a thistle patch. There is a law in the statute book against thistles. There was, and may be now, a law in Connecticut, that "a man should not kiss his wife on ye Sabbath day." It is very easy to make laws, but how about enforcing them?

Struggling through the thistles, taking care to keep within hailing of each other (otherwise there might have been more lost), they came upon the rocky bed of a small stream, and went stumbling on, over large stones and small stones, and going around stones, and, in fact, it was all stones. And here a great diversity of opinion arose, was this small stream the Brook? or should they follow the larger stream?

They followed the smaller, now shut in by high banks, and with the mental certainty on the part of at least one that they were all wrong, were going wrong, and must be wrong, they turned a projecting cliff, and lo! "The First Fall of Lick Brook." The larger stream was afterward, by consulting "the oldest inhabitant," found to be "the Inlet"— the Inlet of Cayuga Lake.

Exclamations of surprise and rapture followed. "Beautiful," "Lovely," "Is this Lick Brook?" "How glad I am I came," "What a nice place for dinner." And it was lovely, a circular basin shut in by wall of rock, a little water falling in cool spray over green and mossy rocks straight down to the bed of the stream below. The most venturesome knew at a glance they could go no further. The "Fall" was unscalable, insurmountable, and they all sat down on the broad, cool, rocky floor, to wonder and admire.

When the stream is high (as afterward seen), and pours over a flood of spray, falling like a veil, it would seem that the nymph of the stream was sporting in bridal robes.

"Another Fall?" "The Upper Fall?" "How can you get there?" And wondering glances at the the walls of rock attested the consternation of the party.

Rested and refreshed (and regaled with fragrant birch, by one of the junior members, who had not as yet left his youth far back), they retraced their footsteps, and stood at the foot of a mighty Hill. A Hill? surely a mistake. Not long since a little girl of twelve summers, in coming from the opposite direction, exclaimed, "Auntie, must we go over that mountain before we get to Ithaca?" And this was the mountain. Formidable it looked; but with brave hearts, and resolute looks, and long drawn breaths, they essayed to climb. The strongest and most determined went ahead, and with the exhortation to "keep in file," and "make a path as you go," they went "onward and upward." Short skirts and no encumbrances, and soon the bushes were loaded with cloaks, capes, mantles, and parasols and all the extras. It was hard work; but a hand occasionally held out from before, and an energetic push from behind, encouraged the lingering and laggard. One after another they dropped down to rest in an open space near the bank, and to take note of each other's haps and mishaps. Breath taken, and a chance to look about, and down, right down below was the Fall they had left.

Upward and onward, an occasional pause for breath, a little time to rest, to grumble, to remark on the weariness of pleasure seeking, to wish impossibilities. The invalid gave signs of despair, could go no further; but encouraged and persuaded, perhaps threatened also (for there was one who carried arms), still struggled on, and the top of the mountain was gained.

Here one gave out entirely, and becoming deaf to entreaties and remonstrances, the ties of friendship and family affection, was reluctantly abandoned to his fate. The invalid still kept on. "O! you leader of forlorn hope, what do you deserve for having inveigled me into this?"

Downward now, down to the bed of the stream. It is easier to go down than up. You have only to shut your eyes and fall as far as possible, it will not be very far, for the low branches of the trees shut in on every side and arrest your progress. The invalid groaned; but looking down saw that one enterprising individual had already gained the desired haven, and was bathing his brow in the the cool water. The effect was electric. Water treatment was that invalid's hobby, and she paused not again, until she was herself under treatment.

In the bed of the stream again. Shut in by walls of solid rock on one side, and on the other by a steep wooded bank; woe to one who should attempt to climb it. The cool water murmured with a pleasant sound, and overhead was a glimpse of the blue sky, and the pleasant outer day.

Following up the ravine, very pleasant and easy, and stooping under the trunk of a gigantic tree, that extended from bank to bank, at the right is a deep chasm, tunnelled out by winter frosts and melting snow, and summer showers dripping through the "jointed structure of the rock."

Still onward, forgetting fatigue and all the other ills of life in wondrous admiration, and suddenly — "the Great Fall." Words are powerless. One by one they sink down on the firm rock floor, to gaze and wonder at the "Beautiful Fall," "Beautiful Fall."

"A thing of beauty is a joy forever."

Falling straight down from the upper air, and the sunlight and the world above, broken only by the slight projection of a strata of harder rock near the base, the bright mountain stream comes down, down, broken into white mist and spray, robes for a hundred water-nymphs.

"Noon glows on the Lake,
Noon glows on the fell,
Awake thee, awake,
White Maid of Avenel."

How high? Ah! none can climb that steep, straight cliff. Rock bound and enchanted, — was that the shadow of Medusa's head?

Taghkanic Fall is 215 feet high, said one. 215 feet, how high is this? If Taghkanic Fall is 215 feet, emphatically remarked the man who carried the pistol, this is, *this is* 250. Proven to a demonstration, carried by acclamation. The act to take effect immediately.

Our geologist was not there, or we should have known the kind of rock, how old, how far back in the "Palæozoic Age," how much older than the coal, and how much younger than the trilobites were its fossils. That is, if a geologist ever gives a direct answer to a direct question. The State geology says it belongs to the "Chemung Group." Very definite that; and the State geology is unquestionable authority, and also says that it abounds in "Felicities." This party, at least, had no reason to disbelieve it. The invalid recovered, and rejoiced again in health and good spirits.

Is it possible that this stream flows from that fountain, to find which Ponce de Leon and his grand cavaliers sacrificed their lives?

The friend left on the mountain was remembered and regretted, but one recalling that he loved Shakspeare well, and knew by heart every "soliloquy," trusted that in that old friend he would find good company.

Slowly, and with long, lingering glances, they bade good-bye to the "Beautiful Fall," went down the glen, drank from the deep pool, and climbed again to upper air. They found their friend, not yet fossilized, gathered up the scattered garments thrown by in the toilsome ascent, and, with the exception of a serious misfortune that befel one of the number (Mem., never wear paper collars to Lick Brook), reached in safety and excellent spirits the foot of the mountain. They were here rejoined by the "lost one," in a state of great indignation. He had not found trout, nor a pretty girl, nor "any peaches," nor any other good thing; had been talked back to by a saucy boy, and was excessively indignant at having been deserted.

Luncheon. Ah, how good it was. The chickens and the ripe tomatoes, and the bottle, and the pears, and all the other good things, and — away.

Beautiful waterfalls, beautiful day, kind friends and true, they will be a pleasant memory forever.

It has been ascertained that when the present elderly

people of the burg of Ithaca were young, they were in the habit of visiting Lick Brook, but not bringing up their children to follow in the footsteps of their fathers (that is not the custom now), it was forgotten. Having been recently rediscovered, they have recalled their lost youth, its pleasures and pic-nics, and also the memory of Lick Brook.

SIX MILE CREEK.

SEEK one of the golden October or Indian summer days, and visit Six Mile Creek, prepared to make a day of it. Go not when the water is high, for then the interest will not be heightened, while the obstacles will be greatly increased. Walk or drive along the south side road, till you come nearly to the Bridge, then descend into the Ravine. On rounding the hill you find yourself in an amphitheatre of vast extent and of a wild and desolate beauty; at the farther end a cataract foams down a pile of irregular rocks. This charming little Fall about fifty feet high is usually called "The Well Fall," in allusion to a phenomenon usual in these streams where the action of the water has gradually worn away deep round holes in the rock. But as there is little or no evidence of these at this spot, whereas there is the largest and most distinctly defined well in all this region at the Upper Falls, soon to be described, the name must have been erroneously from the latter to the former, and as this would leave the present Fall without a cognomen, we take the liberty of

SIX MILE CREEK,—FIRST FALL. ITHACA.

From Photograph by J. C. Burritt.

applying to it that of a citizen, and call it the Cornell Fall. That name already become world wide in its fame, and destined to an immortal renown in the records of philanthropy and education, it is the delight of every Ithacan to inscribe alike on monuments of nature and of art. In time of low water the side of the Fall furnishes a convenient staircase for ascending from the Glen; at other times one is fain to retrace his steps. In either case you return to the point where you left the road before, and scale the abrupt and partly excavated sand bank which overhangs it on the other side. The narrow tongue of land on which you now stand with the deep gully on one hand, and the creek sounding far down on the other, was once a sort of loop or knot hole in the stream, the gully aforesaid being evidently an obsolete channel. Looking back you command a lengthwise view of the wide and desolate glen, through which from side to side meanders the Six Mile Creek, and through the opening at the further end you have a picturesque glimpse of a portion of the village with the gleaming lake and the cultivated hills beyond.

Follow the edge of the Ravine on your left, and you are straightway in a scene of great seclusion, only marred by the ravages of the unromantic axe. In these days, whatever might have been true in ancient times, a man is not "famous according as he lifteth up axes upon the thick trees." To wander close by the stream must formerly have been a very delightful thing, but it is better now to keep within the remnant of woods that the all devouring saw mill has condescended to leave. The high bank, however, affords some interesting views of the glen beneath, as well as many a pleasant spot to while away a half hour luxuriously with a book, such as shall inspire, but not absorb your meditation. The glen is very wide in places on account of the windings of the stream, which will occupy a mile in its twistings and doublings in order to proceed a quarter of that distance, a striking emblem, in all but its gracefulness and beauty, of the career of many a tortuous trafficker in the interest of his country and the votes of his fellow citizens!

Following the wood road which opens before your feet, you presently find yourself in a labyrinth of wild and lonely dells, each of which attracts your romantic spirit. But resisting temptation (only perhaps turning aside to scale the Round Top on your right for the view), you descend to the bank of the Creek, just where it brawls among the rocks at that stage of its career which may be called the Rapids. The woods hereabouts are shady and delightful, and slope gently to the water's edge. A little farther on they expand into a level field bordered on three sides by the Creek. Here is one of the favorite haunts of the writer, and a grand spot for a picnic, or at least a halt. If you would drink in the true aroma of woods and water-brooks, sit down somewhere on one of these old logs and listen, as the season may be, to the singing of birds or the chirping of squirrels (I never saw, by the way, so many of these last most lovable of all wild things, as on this Creek. I am almost tempted at times to christen it anew with the equally descriptive and much more romantic name of Squirrel River). The water chords are so exquisitely stretched over the pebbly bottom, that their music seems to me the softest and most tuneful I ever heard. And the old trees stand around in such graceful attitudes and with such sunny distances between, that there is nothing of gloom, though the whole scene is so primitive and wild, and apparently so remote from human habitation.

On leaving this pleasant Hall of Meditation, a variety

will be added to the excursion by crossing the stream on a bridge of stepping stones, already there, or newly constructed by your own engineering skill. This crossing can be more easily effected, however, by making the detour of the hill and coming down to the stream again, where two giant trees offer their backs as substantial bridges. You continue your woodland walk, the stream beside you now expanding into a great width and trickling through a hundred stony paths, and now narrow, and deep, and still. The opposite side presents every variety of appearance, rocky wall, and shady bank, and towering wooded height. As you approach the narrow Pass, you will be obliged to descend to the edge of the water, where you will find a stone sidewalk, more or less eligible according to your rotundity and agility. The Pass is a narrow defile between the rocks, through which the water pours over a pavement of solid stone. In these clear shallows the minnows are darting to and fro, and the amber, brown, gray, yellow, and green of the rocks beneath, delight the color-loving eye. Altogether this spot is a charming feature of the varied and quiet scenery of Six Mile Creek.

And now on emerging from this cool and shady Pass, do not be discouraged at the axe-desolated and sun-stricken appearance of the scene, for, alas! uncultured cultivation has been here with a vandal hand.

> ——"Nor bate a jot
> Of heart or hope, but still bear up and steer
> Right onward."

And you will yet be rewarded by the best and crowning part of your excursion. To my taste, these reaches of the uninteresting, contribute to the enjoyment of this Creek. In Buttermilk or Enfield there is one continuous vision of beauty; but here the attractions are so dissevered the one from the other, as to unfold before you like the successive scenes of a play, and you enter upon each with a new relish.

Now it will be well for the youthful David of adventure to choose five smooth stones of the brook, for a causeway over the same, if he would slay several Goliath-like difficulties in his path, as well as materially shorten the distance across this open space. The left side of the Creek now becomes, in fact, quite impracticable.

The woods and hills again rise about you, and you go on your way rejoicing under the shade of oaks, cedars and all manner of trees. Across your path a bright cascade comes skipping like a mountain nymph from the hills above. You thread your way, now on a grassy bank, and now, on the pebbly bottom of the stream. After two o'clock of the Indian Summer day, you will see sunset a dozen times behind the hills above you.

The scene suddenly and completely changes as you round a corner, and discover a fall fifty feet in height and of the most curious description. It is situated in a secluded nook that seems expressly fitted up for it. This is the genuine Well Falls, as you may judge by the deep and circular cistern just before you, into which a large portion of the stream pours itself. No graver's hand could have hollowed and smoothed this wonder of nature more deftly than the "continual dropping" of water through countless years. The remainder of the stream has polished the rocks, over which it passes in a thin and foamy sheet, as smooth as marble. The color of the rocks is a deep rich brown, varied by bright green mosses that cling to it under the water so closely as to seem like particles of the stone itself.

Climbing up the stone staircase beside the Fall, you find yourself in a miniature Enfield Ravine, or rather a Lucifer, junior.

The stream narrows into a flume-like channel of solid stone, similar to what, I believe, is called " Lucifer's Bath Tub" at Enfield. A friendly plank conducts you over at this point, and you travel on through one of the wildest, coolest, most rocky of ravines, with the water springing and roaring beside you, and the rocks above filling the narrow pass with premature twilight. Here is a cascade about ten feet high, which raises a roar as you approach it almost equal in volume to Enfield in all its glory. At last the sunlight bursts upon the view ahead, you issue from the ravine and your sight seeing is ended. You take a lane at your left hand, and find your way up to the Green Tree Tavern, where your carriage is waiting, according to previous orders, to convey you back to the village.

THE CASCADILLA.

This is the beautiful and original name of one of our domesticated creeks. Besides this cognominal superiority over its sister streams, it has the advantage of being the most accessible. It is not a wild country beauty, like Taghkanic or Enfield, but trips through our streets like a village belle; yet bursts upon us from the glen with a freshness, and music, and frolic life which many a village belle would share to a far greater degree, if she, too, were oftener seen emerging from the wild and bracing scenes of nature. The Cascadilla is our pet stream.

The banks of the creek, as it passes through the village, are planted with willows. That portion of it which flows through what is called Willow Avenue constitutes one of the most notable features of our "Forest City." For more than half a mile this avenue, consisting of two broad and handsome roads, with the swift and sparkling Cascadilla between, bordered by its parallel rows of willow trees, extends to the Lake. On a pleasant summer evening, when the setting sun is throwing his slant beams across it with a transfiguring glory, and when the roads are alive with citizens on foot, on horseback and in carriages, it presents a highly picturesque and attractive scene to the stranger landing from the steam boat.

The Ravine begins at "Williams's Mill," in the very centre of the village. In fact, at this same point, it was that the first settlers built their cabins, and thence the village grew out in a face-like shape. Within a stone's throw of the entrance of the Ravine, several of these early buildings, retaining more or less of their original appearance, are still pointed out. Passing into the ravine through the Mill yard, you find yourself instantly in a retired spot, which, before the establishment of hog-pens and cow-yards upon its border, must have been an attractive place, as it is the sensation of finding so wild and secluded a spot on the mere turning of a street corner, is worth the courting. There is here, too, a fall, which, notwithstanding the abstraction of so much water from the stream above for the purposes of the mill, furnishes an interesting introduction to our ramble. In thinking what to call it, I am reminded of one, still lingering with us in a ripe old age, who for more than forty years has lifted up his earnest voice like the cataract in the hearing of this community, speaking for God. He needs no monument. His name can never be dissevered from the history and prosperity of Ithaca, but we presume to borrow it to enrich our vocabulary, and would christen this first Fall of the Cascadilla the Wisner Fall.

Crossing the brook on stepping stones (and here it may be well to say that any one afraid of wet feet had better not try the Ravine unless the water is quite low). Keep on the right side of the stream. Presently you turn a corner, and are in a vast, solemn hall of Nature, which would of itself be worth the visit of every contemplative mind. The stream turns two corners in instant succession, forming an amphitheatre at the bend, which strikingly impresses us with the age and power of these floods in wearing away the solid rocks in such deep and graceful curves. Another considerable Fall takes place in the creek as it descends into this amphitheatre. In time of freshet this double bend is the scene of mad and boiling and thunderous excitement, as the floods go plunging through their tortuous bed. Just beyond this second Fall you will be obliged to clamber up the bank. The walk along the brink above, is a favorite one with the writer, especially of a summer afternoon, so shady, so retired and inviting of day-dreams. By and by you find yourself in a grove of pine and hemlock, dim lighted as a cathedral, and carpeted with a clean and fragrant matting from the trees above. The way is now blockaded by a high board fence, and it will be necessary just this side of it to descend again. Several interesting glimpses of the glen and stream below may be gained from the high bank, especially a view of the first cascade, which marks the point where the glen becomes more properly, on account of its narrowing width and wilder scenery, a Ravine. Pouring through the flume of what was once an oil factory on the site of the present Cascadilla Place, and leaping a hundred feet downward from the side of the glen as when the waters burst from Horeb's smitten rocks, the second Cascade is just before you; and on reaching the bed of the stream, it will require a little engineering to pass it dry-shod and unsprinkled. Looking back, hereabouts, a distant view of the village, especially of the gigantic remains of an extinct oil-cloth factory at the Inlet, which contrasts oddly enough with the romantic scenery around.

Looking ahead, your eyes roam refreshingly along a green vista, where the evergreens meet in a pointed Gothic arch above the stream. Directly above you the rocky walls rise, as finely chiseled and as solidly masoned as if by the hand of man, with cedars and pines clinging "for dear life" in the crevices, and perhaps an autumnal forest tree hanging its red flag over the heights. Here and there a tree trunk, mossy and old, has fallen across the path.

Presently you pass through a very narrow portal, where the rocks stand on both sides like the buttresses of some great castle wall. This introduces you to the third of the little cascades, which constitute the peculiar feature of this stream. A little beyond, in the dim shadow of overhanging cliffs and trees, the rocks on your right have been worn into the shape of huge round altars, on which the Giants that warred against the Gods, might have fitly offered penitential sacrifices. The fourth cascade is particularly beautiful, seeming to be made up of a multitude of miniature falls.

And now we come to the third of the Falls, properly so called, of which Cascadilla can boast. We will call it Quarry Falls, from the fact that its present form and size are partly due to the excavations made in procuring the stone for the great Building above. And here we ascend to Cascadilla Place, and inspect its substantial structure, and the magnificent view from its grounds. We take also the only practicable view of the Giant's Staircase, described in our former sketch. A few steps above this wonder of nature, we descend again to the bed of the stream, near the charming cascade No. 5, which like all the rest has beauties of its own. I cannot attempt to describe the loveliness of these sylvan scenes, through which we now pass. They almost make us believe in the wood-nymphs and naiads of old mythology. Certainly these ethereal creatures would have haunted just such spots as these, and would scarcely have startled the rambler had they peered at him through the leafy woods, or flashed upon his sight in the clear streamlet. The green and quiet dell with the sunlight flashing through the trees that join their boughs above, the ancient looking rocks covered with white lichen and long bearded moss, and the gentle streamlet running through the midst, make up one of those ideal scenes which we are apt to think exist only in pictures or in dreams.

We turn a corner, where a splendidly lichened rock juts across the path, obliging us to climb over it to save our feet a wetting, and discover the sixth cascade. These cascades are to the Falls, as asteroids to planets, and if we had not so many full grown cataracts we should esteem ourselves enviably rich in the possession of these. This cascade is a miniature Buttermilk Fall, flowing as it does for a considerable distance over smooth and sloping rocks, and diving with a curling movement into a deep pool. This is a very favorable place for noting the varied and rich coloring of the rocks under water, brown and blue, and purple, and green, and black, and neutral tints indescribable, which no painter's palette may reproduce. Looking onward from this point, we discover another exquisite glade with the evergreen boughs bending down to the stream, which presents a continuous vista of cascades, varying in height from one to three feet. It is a place for the weary heart to rest from " the world, the flesh, and the devil," or if you prefer it from

> "The whips and scorns of time,
> The oppressor's wrong, the proud man's contumely,
> The pangs of despised love, the law's delay,
> The insolence of office, and the spurns
> That patient merit of the unworthy takes."

I leave you to wonder and muse alone, agreeing to meet you at the Dam above. There our limit is reached, and you have your choice to go either by the romantic path to Cascadilla Place, or by the woodland walks which border the north side of the Ravine.

CASCADILLA FROM WILLOW POND.

If you want the most charming and accessible ramble which this Paradise of Rambles affords, walk or ride up to Cascadilla Place. After drinking in a soul full of glorious scenery, made up of hill and valley, Lake and Village, forest and fruitful field, blue sky above, and verdurous landscape threaded by silver creeks and bathing in sunlight beneath, betake yourself to the margin of the Ravine a little below the Buildings. In fact, it were well to proceed some distance till you reach the extreme edge of a jutting cliff from which you can look up the Glen.

Beneath you is a scene of great wildness. The gorge is here deeper than at any other point on the stream, and so narrow that the opposite Bank seems almost near enough to leap upon. At some such spot a Bridge is soon to span the chasm, adding alike to the picturesqueness of the same, and the convenience of the visitor. Before you stretches away the wild and lonely glen, fringed with great pines and cedars, which seem in the immense proportions of the rocks to which they cling, like ferns and shrubs. The white sheet of here and there a cascade, illuminates the somber shades below, and out of the side of rocks on the right leaps a jet of spray, like some fugitive water nymph escaping from an amorous Satyr. It is truly a scene for a painter.

You now return as near the brink as a prudent regard

to life and limb will allow, till you reach another jutting cliff, so covered with low trees as to form a delightful bower, whence you obtain a full front view of the principal Fall of which Cascadilla can boast. If names of natural objects ought to correspond to their appearance, so as to furnish a description in a word, we are at no loss here to call this Fall the Giant's Staircase, for the water tumbles down as regular pair of stairs as ever did the small servant in Dickens's *Curiosity Shop*, and if it does not succeed better than did that self-sacrificing domestic in waking up the stout gentlemen who visit this locality, it will be because they are not intent on the Punch and Judy shows of social life, that there is no love of nature left in them. A little farther on, a cliff just over the Fall, affords a still different view. Here you may not only gaze downward at the Cataract, but look down one of the wildest parts of the glen, and just above, a charming cascade bursts out of the overhanging woods and rocks. If you are geologically inclined, the rock on which you stand, which is one of the most fossiliferous in this region, will yield to your hammer an abundance of specimens, characteristic of the Chemung Group, that composes nearly all our rocks.

Leaving this interesting spot, you walk straight up to the Willow Pond, formed by the accumulated waters of what was once a mill race, and margined by that most amphibious of trees. Your path now lies along the Dyke which borders the Pond and the little gurgling rivulet which feeds it, till you reach the *Ultima Thule* of your ramble. This is a true Lover's Walk. Above you the branching trees, in summer affording an arbor of shade, and filled with singing birds, and now and then a darting and chattering squirrel; at your right hand a little rapid stream, clear and crystal, and musical as a happy heart, and on the other side the wooded slope, that forms the right bank of the Cascadilla, whence an undertone of sonorous melody comes up through the leafy shade, and an occasional gleam of the glen or stream breaks upon the sight.

The path along which you walk is as level and good as the pavements of the town. Commend me to this walk when I would think bright and healthy thoughts, or would hold sweet council with my friend.

You are stopped at last by a most prosaic thing, the Dam. Gentle reader, do not be annoyed, our young men must eat, as well as dream dreams and see visions. There is poetry to the healthy mind in the abundance of bread for the hungry. Besides, this Dam is not altogether devoid of the picturesque itself; and is placed beyond the noteworthy portion of the stream. Exercise your ingenuity in finding the most convenient place to cross the stream, and clamber up the opposite bank, and you are in the woods. If you have a stray copy of Bryant in your pocket, sit down on the first mossy stump and read his "Forest Hymn," or "Inscription for the entrance to a Wood," then in calm and musing enjoyment wander on beneath the branching trees, so interspersed with evergreens, that winter scarcely brings a change over the scene. The ground is richly carpeted with moss, of five or six varieties, and the wild flowers of Spring, the Trifolium, the Columbine, the trailing Arbutus, and many another grow no where more luxuriantly. The squirrels run almost under your feet, and the birds mingle their shrill treble with the base of the Cascadilla. You catch glimpses of the Falls, and of the distant village. You find something new to admire in every fallen trunk. You stoop to drink of the clear cool spring that gushes out from the roots of a great tree. If you wish a purely woodland walk, you take the right hand path, if not you keep as near as possible to the Ravine. You emerge at last in view of the residence of Ezra Cornell, in whose grounds you have been wandering as in your own, and return to the village through the Cemetery, whose beauty and solemn associations furnish a fitting transition to the busy streets beyond. The Cemetery in fact, is worthy of a separate visit. Although covering but 16 acres and therefore not to be compared in size to many others, its natural advantages, in the variety of its surface, and its native growth of trees, and above all its commanding views, make it an object of admiration to all visitors, and the place of all others for the dead to sleep, and the living to meditate. The best view of Ithaca, because the nearest and the most vivid, is obtained from the Fireman's Monument. You look directly down upon the roofs and chimneys, and can hardly escape wishing yourself a Mephistopheles, with power to look through into the domestic life going on beneath. It is certainly suggestive of the truth, that our truest, clearest, and most impressive view of life can only be gained from the standpoint of Death.

14

CAYUGA LAKE.

Among the many acknowledged attractions of, and in the vicinity of Ithaca, the bright clear waters of Cayuga Lake loom up in bold prominence in the back ground of the picture, as seen from any of the lofty eminences almost encircling the village.

At the matin hour of a flowery day in June, spread out at your feet and stretching away off to the north until they mingle with the misty line of the horizon, that has its boundary over the more lordly Ontario, there they repose as quietly as if neither the gentlest zephyr or borean blasts ever disturbed the mirror-like surface of the Lake. And at such an hour the mild cerulean blue of the sky is painted upon it with a softness and delicacy of tone that mortal artist can never hope to equal, and the daintiest tint of the emerald for the time being is dethroned. Linger awhile, and you shall see the hue of the empyrean like a dissolving view, fade imperceptibly away, brightening anon into the most delicate green, and this in turn give way for the sombre limning of the lowering rain cloud; the recent glassy motionless expanse is seen to be ruffled occasionally by those little puffs of wind, the *arant couriers* of the quickly following gale, and the stormy winds begin to blow. This typical infant, repose, that seemed sweetly slumbering in his cradle of flowery fields and sloping banks is aroused, and putting off the habiliments of motionless serenity, seems rapidly transformed to the giant proportions of fabled Eolus, careering high above and around, as if a very demon of destruction. Then does our hitherto fair and gentle Cayuga impress us with vague ideas of the grand, the fearful and the terrible, and then do her foaming crested waves seem mad with frantic efforts to rival their kindred billows of the " vasty deep."

Who among us but loves to steal away for awhile from the dull, stern realities of life, and commune with nature at her own altars — to receive inspiration from her own high priests. So eloquently addressing us in the low murmuring of the west wind, making sweet music in the lofty tree tops — or thundering in our ears in the storm, the tempest, the rushing cataract and the wild rolling flood; so photographed upon our perceptions in the placid lake, the lofty mountain, or the boundless ocean. And who that was ever moved by influences of such a character, can wonder that the swarthy and benighted Asiatic should worship the sacred Ganges, or that the settlers on the banks of the majestic Hudson should almost adore it, or that we, who daily look upon the fair Cayuga should love her, and never tire in singing her praises.

But Cayuga Lake possesses other attributes than those, as seen through the prismatic lens of the poet. A great highway of commerce — bearing upon its broad bosom the products of the field, the forest, the mine and the manufactory. It claims our attention as good business men, and challenges our highest admiration when observed from a merely economic stand point of view. Deep, varying from one hundred to four hundred feet; broad, ranging from one and a half miles at Ithaca, to where, as at Aurora, it expands to a breadth of nearly five miles, and on a misty day is no bad reminder of the great Salt Sea; navigable at nearly all seasons of the year, uniform in volume, ever and slowly moving northward till its waters mingle with and lose their identity in the yet vaster and deeper Ontario — connecting the great Erie with the N. Y. Central Rail Road, and passing through the richest farming lands in the country for forty miles, and with other attributes of sterling value, *why* should it not be prized at its true worth? So then, while the lover of the beautiful and the sublime, delights to gaze upon it from hill top and sloping lawn, to take note only of its value as a vast and exquisite picture, the man of commerce looks down upon this inland sea through a very different medium. To such men, come up before the mind's eye, visions of magnificent steamers, with their priceless freights of humanity; the white winged sloop and schooner, and that *chef d'œuvre* of marine architecture, the plodding canal boat. Behind these visions, and separated but by a gossamer curtain, stands the persistent *will*, that transforms these vagaries of the imagination, as if by the touch of magic, into substantial, tangible realities. A passing moment upon the log book of time intervenes, and lo! like Minerva from the brain of Jupiter, we see leaping from their ways, the Kate Morgans, the Auroras and the Sheldrakes, and as they go to and fro, up and down the bright waters, the astonished denizens of Cayuga's dark depths are frightened from their usual fishy propriety. Scanning the horizon we see those winged messengers of trade, the Gulielmas, the J. Prices and the Nymphs — obeying an unseen power, astound the rustic, who standing upon the breezy shore, looks unutterable things, and almost doubts the evidence of his own senses, while he sees them moving with crested bow and lengthened wake right into the "teeth of the wind." And then again following the tortuous windings of the classic Inlet, we see a long line of canal boats meandering up and down that stream obedient to the steam tug, the Bucephalus of the tow-path, or perhaps, like the Commercial Bank of Clyde, with Admiral Tilton in command, running square before the wind, provided always, a hurricane has sufficient power to overcome her modeled inertia.

Cayuga Lake is peculiarly valuable to another and a very worthy class; to those who see beneath its shiny waves, the haunts of the delicious trout and the noble pike, the black bass and the golden perch. It is valued by him who "knoweth where the bullheads hide," to they who drop their lines at random, or that large and energetic class who draw their nets to Leonard's pebbly shore. And there is still another class of men, who though not numerous, are not the less enthusiastic in their love and appreciation of this superb sheet of water. Your gallant yachtsman looks upon it, and as his practical eye runs over the scene, he sees a great watery plain, whereon contending yachts enter the lists, and with every appliance of art brought to bear upon the modeling of faultless hulls — with the skill and daring of the most expert navigators, they strive in honorable competition for the silver cup, the richly chased pitcher, or the far reaching telescope. He who can witness a spirited and well conducted Regatta, favored with a good twelve knot breeze, and not find therein a source of refined pleasure, lacks something, in the general "make up" of the man; and in the golden chain that unites the nobler and more genial qualities of our nature, if the smallest of the links, you strike one.

"Tenth or ten thousandth, breaks the chain alike." These men who love the foaming billow, and to whom there is no sweeter music than that performed by the winds as they whistle through masts and cordage — well remember the days when the "Ada" tore the chaplet of victory from the fleet keeled *Union* of Geneva in one of the best contested regattas ever witnessed upon our waters, and again and still more decidedly on the deep dark Seneca. They look forward to a coming time when with swifter keels and "foemen worth of their steel," the anticipation of other and greater triumphs shall eventuate in fruition.

The Ithaca Yacht Club, in a Shakesperian sense, may be considered the Prospero of Cayuga and our "rightful duke of Milan," and in a Bennett, they perceive the similitude to a certain imaginary extent, to the great Poet himself, for did they not both create an *Ariel* ready at the bidding of a Prospero; or the said Club, to fly to the uttermost parts of the universe or Cayuga, "and fetch *dew* from the still vex'd Bermoothes" of Aurora Bay or Port Renwick?

To the leisurely traveler and the pleasure seeker, a sail up or down this beautiful sheet of water can but be a source of real gratification. Stop on the trip down, eight miles from Ithaca, at Goodwin's Point, and that awful chasm at Taghkanic Falls shall fill you with wonder and delight. Proceed on, and Aurora, "loveliest village of the plain" gems the east bank of the Lake, twelve miles south of Cayuga bridge, and almost any fine day in summer, or even as late as gorgeous October, a yachtsman may not pass within a marine mile of a line drawn from Long Point to Levanna, but the "Sentinel" will hail him with a sailor's welcome, to drop anchor under the (champaign?) guns of Castle Bogart, or bid him "God speed" on to his place of destination. Springport, six miles farther to the northward will well repay a visit. The Union Springs are enough if we only *hint* at the lurking danger of rosy cheeks and flashing eyes. Proceeding six miles further on, you are at Cayuga, your journey terminates, and the Lake and the graceful, commodious steamer are exchanged for the snorting, rushing Locomotive. This is but a brief and imperfect pen picture of Cayuga Lake in some of its aspects of poetic beauty, commercial value and adaption to aquatic sports. Those well acquainted with its long reaches of semicircular cultivated shore, its outlying points and headlands, its shady banks and rocks rising precipitously from the watery depths, will feel and know the painter's brush has not laid on the colors with a too lavish hand, either in force or brilliancy. That the citizens of Ithaca should wish to share their feelings of pride and gratification with the world at large, when they feast their eyes upon, or sail over this highway of wealth, is but very natural. Time and space will not permit more than an allusion to the traditions of the subject of this sketch, rich as it is in material. The genius of a Cooper is only necessary to erect upon strong foundations of *fact*, superstructures of thrilling romances of the aboriginal days of Cayuga Lake.

TAGHKANIC FALL.

From Photograph by J. C. Burritt.

THE BRIDAL VEIL OF TAGHKANIC.

On the brow of the delicate streamlet,
   In the folds of its forest hair,
I see the gems of a bridal,
   The pearls of a peerless pair.

The rill of the shadowy woodland,
   Runs to the Lake with a spring:
The Indian maid, Taghkanic,
   Weds the Cayuga King.

In the shade of the murmuring maple
   Wait, fair girl, at my side,
Till I lift your wondering lashes
   On the dainty lace of the bride.

Nearer your tremulous footstep;
   Yonder the flash of your eye;
Through the break of the marginal leaflets,
   Where the mist sails up to the sky.

You see it :— I know by the color
   That tells me its rose-red tale:
You see, in the frame of the forest,
   The lace of the bridal veil.

Over the rock it is floating: —
   Is it woven of diamonds or spray:
Of molten pearl or of star-dust? —
   Tell me the fabric, I pray.

You answer me only with dimples
   Hid in a tinting of rose,
And the light of our own near bridal
   Under your eyelid glows.

The Indian maid, Taghkanic,
   Weds with the Sapphire King;—
But a dearer and daintier bridal
   The bloomings of June shall bring.

CORNELL LIBRARY, ITHACA.
From Photograph by J. C. Burritt.

CORNELL LIBRARY.

This Institution, now substantially completed, owes its existence to the public spirit and munificence of Hon. Ezra Cornell, whose name it very appropriately bears. It is located upon the corner of Tioga and Seneca streets in Ithaca; having a front upon the former of sixty-eight feet, and a depth of one hundred. The building is of brick, three stories in height, and so constructed as to be substantially fire-proof.

The idea in which this enterprise originated was to bring within the reach of all classes, freely and without cost to them, the treasures of literature and science; and to stimulate and encourage the intellectual growth of the communities within its influence.

In the accomplishment of this purpose, the clear, practical intellect of its founder foresaw, as the first condition of success, that the Institution should be self-supporting; never a dependent upon the tardy bounty that half aids and half destroys a needy enterprise; but possessing within itself the means of independent existence, and permanent, and sturdy growth. Accordingly, the edifice erected was planned so as to contain, not only the Library and its accessories, but also many rooms so admirably adapted to business purposes as to command, at all times in the future, a large and steadily increasing rental, and thus furnish strength and vitality to the Institution, through the agency of a permanent and durable income.

The execution of this plan met the approval of the entire community. The front of the building, on the first floor, is now occupied by the post office, fitted up with an elegance and convenience rarely excelled; and the First National Bank, whose business rooms, if not as gorgeous as those of the Metropolis, are at least as pleasant and cheerful; while the rear of the building is devoted to offices, all adding their share to the support of the Library. Here also is the arsenal of the De Witt Guards, arranged and adorned with a taste and elegance which does them credit; their drill-room, large and convenient. The Library Hall, a room for public purposes, capable of seating an audience of eight hundred persons, and lighted from the ceiling through globes of glass; the Farmers' Club Room, whose museum of curiosities, and specimens of vegetable growths and mineral formations have become both interesting and valuable; and the Hall of the Historical Society, whose collection, needing only to be arranged and systematized, is rapidly advancing in interest and importance.

From all these sources revenue flows, steadily and ungrudgingly, into the treasury of the Library, making it no dependent upon the charitable impulses of individuals or the public; but able, within itself, abundantly to secure its own existence, and promote its own future improvement. And with the additional aid of the permanent endowments, soon to be made by the liberality of its founder, it will be able to act always independently and with effect, become a recognized power in the community, and largely mould and shape the mental and moral character within the circle of its influence.

Its organization has another commendable element. It is neither sectarian nor partizan. All denominations are represented in its governing Board, and must continue to be. All parties, and shades of parties have equal rights in its management; and the votes of the people which elect a president of the village, the votes of the firemen electing their chief engineer, the votes of the board of supervisors selecting their chairman, directly affect, through these officers, the character and material of the Library corporation. So that no partial or imperfect good is intended; but one that is general, universal, equally open and free to all.

The Library itself is finished with great beauty and elegance. Its alcove-columns represent each of the varieties of our native forest woods. The dark swarthy hue of the walnut, the delicate yellow tracery of the pine, the warm veining of the beach and maple, the red glow of the cedar, the shining panels of the elm, the gnarled heart of the locust, and the hard, white grain of the hickory, and the dusk shadings of the oak; each, with their remaining associates of the forest, combine to make interesting and beautiful, this quiet abode of Literature and Science. Its alcoves are arranged in double stories, and are capable of holding forty or fifty thousand volumes, with a means of expansion and enlargement to any extent which the good fortune of the future may make desirable.

The work of filling these waiting shelves with their silent but eloquent occupants has already begun. About two thousand volumes have been selected and purchased by Mr. Cornell; among which the glowing colors of Audubon's *Birds of America*, and the innumerable plates of the *Inconographic Cyclopædia*, and the old, quaint volumes illustrating the early condition and architecture of London, indicate very clearly his purpose to make the Library collection one of great interest and excellence, and not to be baffled in its execution by even grave questions of expense.

Attached to the Library, and so arranged as to be used in connection with it, are two Reading Rooms, one intended to be exclusively occupied by ladies, and the other by gentlemen; to be open and ready for use at all times; where will be found the newspaper and periodical excellence of the day, and where, it is hoped, a pleasant and cheerful place will be found, to lure the young from the dissipation and revelry of idle days and wasted evenings, to the pleasures of intellectual culture, and genial and improving society.

Much of these results is yet in the future, but the foundation upon which they are to rest is already secure; and the pleasure-seeker who wanders amid the unrivalled scenery which marks the head waters of the Cayuga, when tired of the roar of waterfalls, or cool drip of cascades, or summer murmur of waves, will always find welcome and rest in the quiet and pleasant alcoves of the Cornell Library.

THE CORNELL UNIVERSITY.

BY A. D. WHITE.

In the educational annals of the State of New York the noblest deed by far is the foundation of the University at Ithaca by the Hon. Ezra Cornell.

The General Government had made, in 1863, an appropriation of lands to the different States and Territories, for the establishment of colleges devoted to agricultural, mechanical and other arts and sciences. Of this appropriation the share of New York was very nearly a million of acres.

Of course various parties rushed forward to claim portions of this generous provision. For a time it seemed destined to be scattered among all the institutions known as colleges throughout the State — and that thus the whole fund would be frittered away. But into all this clamor quietly stepped Mr. Cornell, insisted that the fund, to be efficient, must be kept together in one place, and agreed that he would give half a million of dollars to an institution to be established at Ithaca, provided the State should give such institution the income of the new fund.

Despite much opposition, a law was passed chartering the Cornell University, and in September of 1865 the first business meeting of its trustees was held at Ithaca, Gov. Fenton presiding.

Mr. Cornell's promises were far more than redeemed.

He gave into the hands of the trustees not merely the 500,000 dollars, but a beautiful site and farm of over two hundred acres, beside the Jewett cabinet — the most complete of its kind in the country — which had recently cost him ten thousand dollars. Nor did his munificence end here. In accordance with a provision in the charter, he gave $25,000 to found a professorship of agriculture at Genesee College, and invested an additional sum of 50,000 dollars for the University.

The plan of instruction is not yet sufficiently developed to be announced, but while it is intended to begin with a purely agricultural and scientific course, it is not doubted that such course will quickly expand into a large and complete university.

The plans for building embrace large dormitories, lecture and recitation rooms, public halls, library, museum, laboratory, workshops, farm buildings, dwellings, &c. It is intended to erect them from time to time from the interest of the Cornell fund, as they may be needed. It is agreed that while the buildings ought to be substantial and tasteful, there shall be no attempt at display.

The general arrangement will be in large quadrangles, as most convenient and effective.

The site is of surpassing beauty. A plateau over three hundred feet above the level of Cayuga Lake, bordered on one side by the Cascadilla and on the other by Fall Creek, gives a noble place for the buildings and ornamental grounds.

Back of these is the great college farm, on either side are ravines, rocks and falls of water, combining not less beautifully than those at Trenton.

In front, stretching far to the right as eye can reach, are the beautiful waters of Lake Cayuga, — directly in front is the tidy and thriving village of Ithaca, its spires and towers rising amid masses of foliage — and to the left sweeps a bold range of hills, diversified with groves and cultivated fields and dotted with farm-houses, closing in the whole scene as with the walls of an amphitheatre. It is a seat worthy the ideal which it is believed Mr. Cornell's munificence will make real.

By the terms of its foundation statutes, the University must go into operation by August, 1867.

Of course it is too early to give any complete description of an institution from which so much is to be hoped, but the munificence of its founder, his steady earnestness in pressing on the work, and the coôperation of so many devoted to science and education, afford ample ground for the belief that the Cornell University is destined to become an honor to the nation and a power in it.

CORNELL UNIVERSITY.

ORGANIZATION.

Trustees.

His Excellency, Gov. Reuben E. Fenton,
Lieut. Gov. Thomas G. Alvord,
Hon. V. M. Rice, Sup. Pub. Instruction,
Hon. Horace Greeley, New York,
Hon. Edwin D. Morgan, New York,
Hon. Erastus Brooks, New York,
Hon. Wm. Kelly, Rhinebeck,
Gen. J. Merideth Read Jr., Albany,
Hon. Geo. H. Andrews, Springfield, Otsego county,
Hon. A. B. Weaver, Deerfield, Oneida county,
Hon. A. D. White, Syracuse,
Hon. Charles J. Folger, Geneva,
Hon. Edwin B. Morgan, Aurora.
Hon. John M. Parker, Owego,
Hon. T. C. Peters, Darien.
Hiram Sibley, Rochester.
Hon. Lyman Tremain, Albany,
Hon. Ezra Cornell, Ithaca.
Hon. J. B. Williams, do
Hon. Geo. W. Schuyler, do
William Andrus, do
John McGraw, do
Francis M. Finch, do
Alonzo B. Cornell, do

Officers.

Chairman,   Treasurer,   Secretary,
Hon. Ezra Cornell,   Hon. Geo. W. Schuyler,   Francis M. Finch.

Executive Committee.

William Andrus,
Hon. Josiah B. Williams,
Hon. George W. Schuyler,
Alonzo B. Cornell,
Hon. Edwin B. Morgan,
Hon. John M. Parker,
Hon. Ezra Cornell,
Hon. Thomas G. Alvord,
Hon. Horace Greeley.

Building Committee.

Hon. A. D. White,
Hon. William Kelly,
Hon. Ezra Cornell,
Hon. A. B. Weaver.
Francis M. Finch.

Finance Committee.

Hon. Edwin D. Morgan,
Hon. Josiah B. Williams.
John McGraw,
Hon. William Kelly,
A. B. Cornell.

CORNELL UNIVERSITY.

ORIGIN AND PLAN.

It is intended here merely to sketch the beginnings of an enterprise whose ultimate purposes are so large and grand as to tempt one to luxuriant prophecy rather than sober recital.

A volume which leads its readers in a lengthened stroll among the cascades and cataracts which form the head-waters of the Cayuga, would be sadly incomplete if it gave no hint of the Institution of Learning preparing to rise in their midst and dominate them all.

Therefore, it is proposed to sketch briefly, and it is hoped, coolly, the origin and aim of the Cornell University.

To speak very generally, it proposes to accomplish in the higher walks of learning, what our free school system has nobly and successfully done in the rudimental branches; to afford to the poor scholar, struggling to educate himself up to high standards of acquirement, the precise opportunity which he needs, and so to place all upon a level, that within its walls there shall be no aristocracy of Family or Fortune, but only that of Brain.

It originated in the years of war. The waste of treasure and of life in crushing rebellion, did not paralyze, but only strengthened the purpose of its founder. There seemed to him only the more terrible need of a widely diffused and thoroughly disciplined intelligence.

Congress had granted to the several States a princely inheritance of public lands to be devoted to educational purposes. The portion falling to the State of New York represented about one million of acres. Our legislature had given this magnificent donation to an institution already in existence, upon certain special conditions, framed to ensure results commensurate with the splendor of the gift. Those conditions were not performed; no sure guaranty of their fulfillment in the future could be obtained; and in this emergency a senator rose in his place at the Capitol and proposed to give two hundred acres of land and half a million of dollars to found a University. This, in the midst of a desolating war, bravely indicated the strength of the American arm, and the courage of the American heart.

Difficulties however sprang up. Other existing institutions of learning asked for portions of the congressional grant; but the evil of dividing and so dissipating the fund became so plainly apparent, that in the end all magnanimously yielded the advancement of their own interests to the purpose of building up one grand, central University, to which the gift of the nation and the endowment of its founder should be given unbroken;—all, except one. The gift of land and of money was permitted to be made upon a condition which reads thus in the Act of Incorporation:

"Provided further, that no such payment shall be made unless within six months from the passage of this Act, said Ezra Cornell of Ithaca shall pay over to the Trustees of Genesee College, located at Lima in this State, the sum of *Twenty Five Thousand Dollars* for the purpose of establishing in said Genesee College a professorship of Agricultural Chemistry."

This condition was fulfilled. The money was paid to "the Trustees of Genesee College located at Lima:" they accepted it "for the purpose of establishing in said

Genesee College a professorship of Agricultural Chemistry." May the result be all that the warmest advocates of the measure can possibly have anticipated!

Having thus complied with this preliminary condition, the founder of the University was left at liberty to give away a half million of dollars. This was done promptly, and the Trustees of the Institution, men of state and national reputation in large proportion, at once entered upon their duties.

The location decided upon is one of rare excellence. All who have read the descriptions of this volume will recall the scenery of Fall Creek and the Cascadilla; the one a chain of cataracts, the other of cascades. Between these two streams, upon the slope of an eastern hill are the grounds of the University. In the valley at the north is the long, blue line of the Lake, bending gracefully around green headlands and pebbly points, and melting into the sky in the far distance. Below are the spires, and clustered dwellings, and shaded streets of the village; and beyond the horizon is barred by the rise of the Western hill, dotted with rural homes, and green with the promise of spring, or golden with the ripe wealth of summer. Far at the south glides away a winding valley, buttressed on either hand by silent hills and hiding in its bosom a brawling stream, whose route is marked by a misty haze. On every hand nature presents all her beautiful variety, and the eye is never weary with the changeful landscape.

Here the labor of a century is to begin. The artisan is at work. Lofty observatory, graceful library, spired chapel, massive dormitory, tasteful cabinet,—these are yet in the future slowly to grow into being and beauty, and swarm with the busy youth of the State in the coming time. The rest is prophecy. It is better to leave that to the swift unfolding of the years. Only this is sure, that back of and behind this enterprise stands the firm will and dauntless purpose that spoke it into life, with every noble energy and unselfish impulse chrystallizing about it; determined, if life be spared, to see it fully accomplish the highest destiny marked out for it; and to make it at once the pride, the glory and the safeguard of the State.

THE MANUFACTURING FACILITIES OF ITHACA.

BY E. CORNELL.

The elements of cheap power is the first essential necessity for manufacturing. The facility for reaching market through cheap and reliable avenues is the next important consideration. Then follows the questions of cheap building materials, cheap and abundant food, cheap labor, and facilities for procuring the raw materials to be manufactured advantageously and with certainty.

These several advantages center naturally at Ithaca, as will be seen by a reference to the details of the subject. Water power is found on Fall Creek which passes through the northern portion of the village, to the extent of 500 feet perpendicular fall, in one and a half mile length of the stream, and all within a mile and a half of the post office. The minimum power of each 25 feet of this fall is sufficient to drive a flour mill of eight runs of stones. There are two other streams passing through the village which afford half as much more power. Of this vast power, eighty per cent. is idle, and seeks occupation at nominal prices.

Steam power: This the more important element of manufacturing power, as it is capable of indefinite multiplication, can be produced cheaper at Ithaca than at any other place in the State on navigable waters. This cheapness will be at once understood when it is mentioned that an investigation on the subject of the Ithaca and Towanda rail road, now in progress of construction, which was made in the summer of 1865, resulted in proving that the coal from the Barckley mines (at the prices then prevailing for mining, dressing and fitting the coal for market, an allowance of fifty cents a ton as a royalty for the coal in the mine, and rail road transportation to Ithaca, a distance of 65 miles), could be laid down at Ithaca for a cost of $2.50 per ton. In seasons of ordinary prices, this coal could be placed at Ithaca at a cost of $1.75 per ton. The amount of developed coal, in and near the Barckley mines, exceeds fifty millions of tons. Such facts present a source of unlimited power, at the lowest possible rates. The anthracite coal also reaches Ithaca cheaper than at other points in the State, except Binghamton and Owego.

The facilities for reaching market is afforded by the New York and Erie railway, the Delaware, Lackawanna and Western Rail Road, by the steamers on Cayuga Lake, and New York Central R. R., and by the Erie Canal. A rail road which is soon to connect Ithaca with Sodus Bay and Oswego will greatly increase these facilities. It is also expected, at no distant day, that the Cayuga Lake will be connected to Lake Ontario by a ship canal, which will open the entire chain of lakes from Ogdensburg to Chicago and Superior City, to vessels hailing from the port of Ithaca. With this improvement, Ithaca becomes a point where the coals of Pennsylvania, and the ores of North-eastern New York, Canada and Lake Superior can be brought together at less cost than at any other point, thus giving Ithaca superior advantages for the various manufactures of iron and copper. A large traffic would soon grow up between Ithaca and the ore supplying regions on the great lakes, they requiring the cheap coals from Ithaca, and Ithaca in turn taking their ores, thus affording tonnage both ways, which produces the greatest economy in transportation.

The investigations which resulted from the building of the Cornell Library, and the effort to secure the location of the asylum for the blind at Ithaca, demonstrated, that building materials were cheaper at Ithaca than at any other place of equal population in the State, and that manufacturing buildings could be erected there at twenty per cent. less cost than at other localities.

The same is the fact in reference to food and labor. Ithaca is surrounded by an excellent agricultural district of mixed products, from the grain and the dairy farms, and with a population of industry and thrift, which would supply a large amount of help for any class of manufacturing.

Ithaca is also one of the finest fruit districts in the State, which will add largely to the luxuries as well as the cheapness of living. Thus it will be seen, as fully as can be shown in a brief article, that Ithaca possesses desirable, cheap and enduring facilities, for a prosperous manufacturing town.

ITHACA IN 1834.

BY SOLOMON SOUTHWICK.

The following extract is from a pamphlet, written thirty years ago, by the late eccentric and talented Solomon Southwick:

ITHACA, *September* 11*th*, 1835.— When I visited Ithaca last year, I had no expectation of returning, unless it should be merely to pass through on a tour among the southern tier of counties on the west side of the Hudson: But events, in the order of Providence, having brought me once more as a sojourner, to this delightful, if not enchanting spot, where the God of Nature has been so lavish of his bounties, and where Art is yet destined to behold some of her noblest triumphs; I have been induced, at the request of several gentlemen, to copy for the press, some particular views of the scenery and water powers in ann about Ithaca, which I took during my former visit; inasmuch as they may lead the distant reader to form clearer views of the future prospects of this beautiful and interesting village.

I am no landscape painter, and have never been in the habit of descriptive composition; but had I the genius of Claude Loraine, as a painter of natural scenery; and that of Shakespeare, Milton, or Thompson, as poetical describers of such scenery, I should still despair of doing anything like ample justice to the uncommonly beautiful landscape views; the grand and numerous waterfalls; and the sublime height of steep and rugged rock, or verdant mountain top, with which Ithaca is surrounded; and by means of which she is destined not only to become one of the most favorite resorts of fashion, taste, and genius; but one of the most wealthy and flourishing of inland cities; for a city she will become of no small magnitude, long before the rising generation shall have passed away. This prediction is, I think, justified by the details which follow; and that it will be verified, though time must determine this point, I feel as confident as I do that I am now wielding my pen. Nothing can prevent it, nothing will prevent it if her present population possess the necessary enterprise, and take the proper measures, which her local and relative position demands, to bring her into notice, and hasten on her final success. "*Fortune favors the bold,*" was a heathen maxim, and has been often a stimulant with Christians to enterprise and perseverance; but the citizens of Ithaca have only to believe, what is no doubt strictly true, that whatever they undertake for the advancement of their prosperity and happiness with a firm reliance on Divine Providence for success, will be brought to a happy conclusion. God never forsakes any who trust to his promises, and obey his laws: And moreover, where the foundations of human prosperity are so broadly and so deeply laid as they are at Ithaca, the very circumstance is an invitation from the Divine Beneficence to build and improve upon them till all their advantages are completely realized.

AN OLD LAND MARK.

THE ITHACA HOTEL.

Standing on the south-west corner, at the intersection of Aurora and Owego streets, the venerable Ithaca Hotel still looks on with a benignant smile at the gliding throng as they hurry past or crowd its threshold, and here it has stood for the last half century, unchanged and unmoved by the world's turmoil, bustle and progress. Originally erected by Luther Gere, Esq., one of the founders and early pioneers of Ithaca, it was looked upon as a model hotel; and amid all the changes of time, has maintained its early reputation.

Before the days of rail roads and telegraphs, from its front rolled away daily the various stage coaches for Catskill, Utica, Geneva, Buffalo, and the lines running to all points of the compass; and then was gathered in its halls and porticoes the hurrying throngs of a busy and impatient generation; those who then complained of slow coaches, and were not quite satisfied to make the trip to New York in the unprecedented short time of five days, alas! have passed away with the coaches that bore them on, and a new generation has entered into their possession and taken their places, and like their fathers before them, still complain that the rail consumes twelve or fourteen hours of their time in setting them down in Broadway, and seem quite as impatient as were their ancestors at the time-tables of the Swift-sure Line of United States mail coaches, the echoes and dust of whose wheels have long since passed. Few have been the changes wrought by time in the old Hotel; here it stands to-day, venerable in years, but bright in its exterior, and within as of old given to hospitality. Less ostentatious in frescoed ceilings and gilded cornices than its modern rivals, it wears upon its every feature the dignity which time alone can give, and boasts more of memories of the past than promises of its future. Its front pavements have been bored, not for oil; but many a hickory shaft has been put down, and towering aloft with the Stars and Stripes given to the breeze, proclaimed it the "Old Tammany of Tompkins County." Its halls have been packed with untold conventions, and the affairs of the Nation in all its changes, have been discussed by a generation of patriots. Beneath its roof gathered the patriots of 1812, and were mustered into service; here was the roll call for the heroes of 1861, and the the echoes of the traitors' guns had not died away from Fort Sumpter before the citizens of Tompkins gathered at the hearthstone of the old wigwam to offer their money and their lives for the defence of the Union.

Its ceilings have echoed with the eloquence of De Witt Clinton, Silas Wright, Martin Van Buren, and a host of statesmen who have passed away. Venerable old pile! May the dust of Time gather lightly on thy brow.

Under the able management of mine host, Col. Welch, the Prince of Landlords, may the weary who seek thy threshold still find the Ithaca Hotel a home for the stranger, with a genial hand to welcome their arrival. A table of the choicest viands to invite their indulgence and restore their wasted energies, and when the sojourner for a day or month departs thy hospitable shelter, we are sure it will be with pleasant memories, and above all, we are sure it will be with so light a bill as not to materially endanger the bank account of the departing guest; and if regrets are experienced at all, they will be only felt that they cannot delay their visit longer, and enjoy its quiet repose and the urbane courtesies of its presiding spirit, Col. Wm. H. Welch.

CLINTON HOUSE, ITHACA.

From Photograph by J. C. Burritt.

THE CLINTON HOUSE.

In two classes of hotels only, can Shenstone's memorable stranger, which declares that life's fairest welcome is found at an Inn, be fully appreciated. In those snug, cosy, delightful little affairs which were before the rail road era, scattered on all the high roads of England, and in those superb establishments of our own day, when all life's necessities and most of life's luxuries are in the call of the guest.

A great revolution in the conduct of a hotel was made in the administration of Warriner of Springfield, who so suffused his table with delicacies, that a week at his house was a perpetual feast — and no one ever sat at his tea table especially, and was waited on by "Emily" — but that he found a new chapter in the gastronomic life.

Then Boyden of the Tremont initiated new order and discipline, and the standard has been increasing in its degree, till our American hotel life is as near the complete as can be found in the world.

The most imposing and dignified building in all the beautiful plain of Ithaca is the Clinton House. Not even the elegant Cornell Library edifice, is as impressive to the entering traveler. In those massive columns, that broad portico, that proportioned rising of the whole building till its belvidere crowns all, it is evident that the founders of this admirable House, had bold ideas of architectural excellence. It bears the name of *Clinton*, because at the date of its formation, that statesman had in Ithaca enthusiastic friends, who were glad to affix his name to their great effort in enterprise. The people recognized Clinton as the founder of the canal, and the Erie canal unlocked the treasures of the West. This laurel can we never unbind from the brow of that splendid man.

The Clinton House is situated just where good taste would select. In the centre of the village, near its park, directly nigh its business street, on an avenue which runs from the hill side that is the way of the iron road, far down to the beach of the Lake. The situation is that which would now be selected, and this is high praise, when it is remembered how many years have passed since the Clinton House was erected.

The hospitable record of the House is a capacious one. It includes statesmen and jurists, and also of travelers of celebrity who have shown their good taste in journeying, by traversing the regions of the Cayuga. From the venerable Surveyor General De Witt (the friend and correspondent of Washington), who watched its building with so much hope of its success, its register has been graced by thousands of names, good and true, not the least interesting page in which, is that which records the signature of the principal diplomâts accredited to our government, when making with the Secretary of State, their tour of the country.

The rebuilding of the House in 1862, was due to the increased enterprise of Ithaca. Mr. Cornell and Mr. Thompson together planned the new arrangements. They made the house a modern one. It was a stately and capacious one in its old devisings; but it now has in its broader spaces and more beautiful appointments, those ways of living which our more fastidious — more rapid age demands. The characteristics of the Clinton House is its comfortable quiet. It is a home, if but for the night, for the flitting or the abiding traveler, it is the pleasant resting place.

Its dining room does not affect one as over large, but as just the nice apartment in which at a table of suitable size his meal silently and luxuriantly taken in ease. The house is large enough for all purposes, but it is snugly arranged, and the guest is delighted to find that he has found a place where he knows that he is to be cared for, and allowed to do as his own good taste may dictate.

If he ascends to the belvidere, he has before him a picture of prosperity — a pleasant village is at his feet — houses, churches, shop and store are all around him — he sees the Inlet like a small Scottish river glittering in the midst of the verdure of garden and of hill; while in the not far distance, the broad shield of the Cayuga reflects whatever may be the momentary beauty of the shore or of the skies.

The valley rises to easy and agreeable drives. All around the village, scenery of the romance of Swiss ravines and gorges give bold relief to the placid beauty of the plain. The traveler may easily be allured to days of abiding in this pleasant alteration of his in and out door life.

The landlord will care for him and not intrude on him. Of all the disciplined service of his house, Mr. THOMPSON may be the quietest man. He comprehends what the well ordered rules of such a house should be. They are given and obeyed, and he sees that the routine is observed; and in this wise care for the security and ease of his guest, the high reputation of the Clinton House is preserved.

No one that sees what the action of our rapid, urgent, nomadic life in this country is, can doubt the value to a village that seeks to maintain itself in its place of power as a community, of such establishments as is the Clinton House. It gives the ready answer to a question travelers ask, where shall I go? It makes of Ithaca, a desirable mark in the journey, and the tourist calculates his progress by time. These pages of favorable word will be justified by the experience of those who come to Ithaca. They will be but the approved meed of each traveller.

The Clinton House was built from 1828 to 1831. It owes its existence to the large purposed enterprise of Jeremiah S. Beebe, Henry Ackley and Henry Hibbard, gentlemen whose names cannot be dissevered from the history of the progress of Ithaca. They built in advance of their day, but so do all men who dare to do bold and liberal acts. Those were dream like days for building, for the great structure originally cost only ($22,000) twenty-two thousand dollars. The brick cost $2.25 per thousand. The master carpenter received his one dollar twenty-five cents per day — other carpenters and masons from 75 cts. to one dollar per day. Our new forests yielded their lumber in the choicest and best at ten dollars per thousand — the common not five dollars. The times are changed indeed. The new repairs which Messrs. Cornell and Thompson made to the building cost ten thousand dollars. Mr. Morris, who yet survives, was the master builder.

The construction of the stairs was however considered a work of so much difficulty, that the services of a New York artist were procured. Our builders in 1865, would build a staircase to the planets, if the structure could find foundation.

The Clinton House.

The Clinton House in locality succeeds the Columbian Inn — and faint traces of the Revolutionary period can be noticed in this name, as Columbia was a favorite eagleism of our writers and orators in the twilight influences of the war that made us a nation.

Spencer and Dunning opened this house. It stands to-day, of the first class, and prominent in that class, of all the hotels outside of the larger cities. It shall yet, we trust, witness with all that honor the opening banquet, which shall be spread before scholars and thinkers and men of art and full life, to celebrate the completion of the Cornell University.

FIREMAN'S MONUMENT, ITHACA.

The above monument stands in the beautiful cemetery of Ithaca. The lot is for the free burial of any Fireman. From this point there is one of the finest views in the world. The village is below; the Lake at the south, and the hills and valleys at the north and west.

FIREMAN'S MONUMENT, ITHACA.

Photographed by J. C. Burritt.

LICK BROOK.

Spirit of Beauty, and nursling of light,
Phantom in essence, yet potent in might,
The forest depths and tangled wild,
Joy to welcome thee — Nature's child.
To the yearning heart of a lonely nook,
Thou gavest the murmuring, tuneful brook.
Long years have come, and years have gone,
But the song it sang, that brook sings on;
The flowers of Spring still blush at its wooing,
And mosses rejoice at its eager pursuing.

List! the rocks to the rivulet loudly are calling,
While resonant defiles the echoes prolong,
"Come, O thou fair streamlet! no danger appalling,
Shall check the full tide of thy musical song."

"O'er this desolate bosom, no blossoms are flinging,
Their odors from censers of purple and gold,
These rude arms extend, but no tendrils come clinging,
More genial the natures they fondly enfold."

The loitering rivulet, softly revealing,
Its love to the blossoms that smiled at its side,
In hidden recesses, its currents concealing,
Burst forth in the fullness of sympathy's tide.

Then swifter and stronger, the torrent rushed sweeping,
Along its cool margin, fresh verdure unrolled,
It bathed, as it sprang, the stern precipice leaping,
Bald foreheads of granite, grown centuries old.

As years hasten on, thro' the distance resounding,
The waters their spray-wreathed sisters will call,
Whose echoing footsteps in joyous rebounding,
Upon memory's ear shall refreshingly fall.

I have wandered afar, amid ruins enshrouded
In loving regret by the dark evergreen,
The cocoa's shade, and the sunlight unclouded,
And billowy verdure adorned the fair scene.

Over lone, barren deserts, unblest by sweet fountains,
Or pausing to rest by Pacific's calm tide,
Or climbing the steeps of Nevada's grey mountains,
Whose summits uprear in their desolate pride.

In fancy, I've heard the bright waters replying,
To breezes that wander through Ithaca's vale,
As impetuous Youth breathed affection undying,
And warm lips repeated love's own fairy tale.

There are those we have cherished, no longer returning,
Who listened with us to deep Taghkanic's roar,
A mightier anthem they since have been learning
From surges that break on Eternity's shore.

H. N. R.

Oyster Bay, L. I., May 8th, 1866.

BUSINESS LOCALITIES, ETC.

Steamboats from Central Rail Road to Ithaca.

KATE MORGAN, Capt. Goodrich. AURORA, Capt. Dryer.
SHELDRAKE, Capt. Ryerson.

Rail Roads.

DELAWARE and LACKAWANNA, from Erie Rail Road at Owego, to Ithaca; Wm. R. Humphrey, Superintendent.

Hotels.

CLINTON HOUSE, S. D. Thompson.
TOMPKIN'S HOUSE, Holmes & Stamp.
FARMERS' HOTEL, J. B. Scott.
ITHACA HOTEL, W. H. Welch.
FARMERS' EXCHANGE, E. H. Watkins.
LIVERMORE HOUSE, C. Livermore.

Halls.

HALL in Cornell Library. VILLAGE HALL. CLINTON HALL.

Post Office.

In Cornell Library, J. H. Selkreg, P. M.

Schools.

ITHACA ACADEMY, S. G. Williams, Principal. *Female Department*—Mrs. S. G. Williams, Principal.
DISTRICT SCHOOL No. 16, S. B. Howe, Prin. Several private schools.

Ithaca Brass Band.

A. B. Whitlock, Leader.

Telegraphs.

UNITED STATES TELEGRAPH, Miss J. A. Nourse, Operator.
WESTERN UNION TELEGRAPH, J. H. Tichenor, Operator.

Newspapers.

AMERICAN CITIZEN AND DEMOCRAT, Spencer & Williams.
ITHACA JOURNAL AND ADVERTISER, J. H. Selkreg.

ERRATA.

As one of the writers for this work, who has contributed a larger number of sketches than any other, was unable to read the proof while the book was going through the press, it is deemed only justice to him to add the following table of the principal Errata occurring in his articles, which will be corrected in the text of the next edition. The errors were probably made in transcribing the original manuscript by another hand unacquainted with his handwriting.

Page 10, for " extra " read " extreme."
" 11, for " ruinous " read " rimous."
" 12, for " nodose " read " nodosi," and for " Sully " read " Tully."
" 13, for " made an effort " read " made *no* effort."
" 13, the Note belongs on page 95.
" 20, for " descending " read " ascending," and for " gardens " read " garlands."
" 21, insert " you " before " will find."
" 22, for " mills of the Gods " read " mills of God."
" 26, for " sound " read " sounds."
" 29, for " wee things " read " wee thing."
" 30, omit the word " juxtaposition " after the word " line."
" 31, read " opposite, a frowning wall of rock rises," &c.
" 32, for " situation " read " situations."
" 33, for " sufficiently if front " read " sufficiently in front."
" 36, for " 280 " read " 480."
" 87, after " erroneously " insert " transferred."
" 96, for " face-like " read " fan-like."
" 97, after " attractive place " insert a semi-colon, and a comma after " as it is."
" 98, insert " you gain " before " a distant view."
" 102, for " not intent " read " *so* intent."

www.ingramcontent.com/pod-product-compliance
Lightning Source LLC
Chambersburg PA
CBHW030341170426
43202CB00010B/1197